THE PLEASURE OF PRESERVING

INSPIRED RECIPES FOR MAKING YOUR OWN PRESERVES

– SEREN EVANS-CHARRINGTON –

An environmentally friendly book printed and bound in England by
www.printondemand-worldwide.com

Mixed Sources
Product group from well-managed
forests, and other controlled sources
www.fsc.org Cert no. TT-COC-002641
© 1996 Forest Stewardship Council

PEFC Certified
This product is
from sustainably
managed forests
and controlled
sources
www.pefc.org

PEFC/16-33-415

This book is made entirely of chain-of-custody materials

THE PLEASURE OF PRESERVING
INSPIRED RECIPES FOR MAKING YOUR OWN PRESERVES

Copyright © 2014 Seren Evans-Charrington. All rights reserved.

First paperback edition printed 2014 in the United Kingdom

A catalogue record for this book is available from the British Library.

ISBN 978-0-9574438-1-5

No part of this book shall be reproduced or transmitted in any form or by any means, Electronic or mechanical, including photocopying, recording, or by any information retrieval System without written permission of the publisher.

Published by Bubbling Stove Publications
For more copies of this book, please email: hello@bubblingstove.co.uk

Designed and set by Printondemand-Worldwide.com
www.printondemand-worldwide.com

A big thank you to my wonderful parents, who have been supportive in every way possible. Many thanks to Annie and Charlie Jones for their support and attendance of early cookery demonstrations, tasting duties and for allowing me to raid their vegetable patch.
A special thank you to Millie and Monty Jones who are the best food critics on earth and brilliant at pulling up beetroot.
Finally a huge thank you to Layla Long and her family, for their friendship, support and sampling endurance.

Artwork: Medlar Fruit copyright © 2014 Layla Long

Although every precaution has been taken in the preparation of this book, the publisher and author assumes no responsibility for errors or omissions. Neither is any liability assumed for damages resulting from the use of this information contained herein.

Dedication

To my little helpers, Harriet and Olivia who are a constant stream of inspiration and distraction to my writing, but a joy to watch grow.

Contents:

Foreword

This book is designed for anyone who is starting out on their preserving journey or wants to improve the results of their preserve making. It is not an exhaustive guide, but it is written in the hope that it will provide a bit of an historical backdrop for the subject and a good foundation knowledge and understanding of this ancient art.

I hope that the recipes in this book will trigger childhood memories and spark the creation of new ones as you peel, chop and stir your way to wonderful preserves.

About the Author

Tucked away in a corner of Wales Seren Evans-Charrington works as food historian and professional cook. Most weekends she can be found donning a period costume and cooking up delicious treats from the depths of our culinary history.

With two young daughters who are both under five and a menagerie of animals and pets, Seren decided to retreat to the country and try to restore the life work balance. She now juggles period cooking, food writing and family commitments in what she describes as 'chaotic bliss'.

Seren's work is based on a culmination of a real passion for British food history and an obsession with preserving and a love of old cookery books. Her work has seen her make television and radio appearances as well as having won awards for her heritage food range, including being awarded a Bronze for her Bergamot lemon, quince and grapefruit marmalade at 'The World's Original Marmalade Awards' held at Dalemain Mansion in Cumbria.

Introduction

There are some things in life you simply need to know, like jam making is next to homeliness and the gift of jars of chunky fig marmalade will make you popular amongst friends, whilst a store-cupboard of brandied apricots will always ensure a steady flow of visitors.

Home food preservation is a fascinating subject and there are a great many ways that food can be preserved at home, although this book concentrates on the practical methods that the average busy householder with basic kitchen equipment can easily tackle. Whilst techniques to wind dry a fillet of cod or a two-week long recipe to candy tomatoes are fascinating to read it's unlikely that the average home-preserver will get around to trying their hand at them, so this book describes practical ways to bottle your own jam, make marmalade, pickle and chutney your way through the seasons.

Preserving is an age old method that has been employed for centuries to slow down the natural process of decay. Preserving was born out of the necessity to extend the shelf life of seasonal harvests. Through preserving the summer glut of fruit and vegetables could be hoarded away to ensure a supply of food in the bleak winter months. In times past a well-stocked larder was an essential element to survival. In a modern world where the natural seasonality of fruits and vegetables has no bearing on its availability it is easy to forget, that there was a time that there was little protection from the natural order of things and that when a fruit or vegetable was out of season, it simply wasn't available. No soft fruits flown in from hot climates in December or garden peas in October, so you either preserved in the months of plenty to guard against the barren, hungry winter months or you risked going without. In town and country alike preserving was an important and normal part of the household routine.

Today, the desire to bother making preserves is often simply that home-made preserves are delicious and give control over the ingredients. Preserving is a simple art that once mastered can be enjoyed throughout the seasons and there is something deeply innate and satisfying in knowing that the larder is well stocked with home-made preserves. It's hard to explain how preserving fulfils some deep seated nesting instinct, but it does.

The recipes in this book require only basic equipment that can be found in most kitchens. There is no need to invest in fancy preserving pans when a good sized stainless steel pan will do nicely, but what is essential to good preserving is mastering the basic techniques, following hygiene practices and using the best ingredients available to you. To say that bad fruit and vegetables will make bad preserves is stating the obvious, but it is true. The basic rule is that if you don't consider something good enough to eat then don't preserve it.

Once the techniques of preserving are mastered you will find yourself joining the smug ranks of successful home economists and you will never stop finding new ways to capture the flavours of fresh produce.

Let the preserving commence!

Chapter One – The Basics

Hygiene and Food Safety

Basic hygiene rules should be applied when preserving, ensuring that all your work surfaces and equipment are scrupulously clean before you begin and that you sterilise all jars before use.

Good sterilisation is essential for achieving good preserves that last without spoiling. Sterilisation is not complicated but it is required to remove all bacteria, yeasts, fungi and organisms from the jar so that when you use it for preserving, the food will remain fresh once sealed.

Jar Health Check:

Before sterilising jars check the jars thoroughly for damage such as cracks, breaks, and chips. If you find any of your jars are damaged you must discard them.

Next you need to thoroughly wash your jars, inside and out, in hot soapy water and rinse in boiled water.

Once your jars are clean you are ready to choose a sterilisation method:

Sterilisation check list:

1.   It is important that you only sterilise your jars and lids for a short time before you are ready to fill

them to ensure they remain warm for the filling process.

2.   Important: Do not attempt to sterilise your bottles and jars by pouring boiling water into them

3.   Always take care when handling hot jars and lids, please use the appropriate equipment such as jam jar tongs, oven gloves or doubled over thick tea towel.

Method 1: Water Bath

Step 1: Remove the lids from your jars and put to one side. Next place the jars into a large saucepan with lid and fill with water until jars are covered.

Step 2: Slowly bring to the boil and keep at the maximum temperature for 10 minutes, turn the heat off and cover the pan to keep the jars warm until you are ready to fill them.

Step 3: Place lids in a small pan and fill with enough water to cover, heat and simmer for 10 minutes, turn the heat off and cover the pan until you are ready to seal the jars.

Method 2: Oven

Step 1: pre-heat oven to 140∘C/ 275∘F/Gas Mark 1

Step 2: Wash jars and lids thoroughly in hot water and then transfer immediately to pre-heated oven for fifteen minutes.

Step 3: Keep warm in the oven until ready for filling.

Method 3: Dishwasher

Step 1: Remove the lids from your jars and place everything into the top rack of your dishwasher and run it on a hot wash. No detergent or cleaning solutions should be used.

Step 2: Time your dishwasher cycle to finish just as you are ready to fill the jars or leave the jars and lids or seals inside the dishwasher to keep warm until you are ready to fill them.

Spoilers: Enemies of the Preserver

You could make the most wonderful preserve in the world, but it will be a futile exercise if you do not eliminate the microorganisms also known as spoilers, namely, Enzymes, Bacteria, Mould and Yeast. If you are armed with knowledge of these spoilers and how to control them then there is nothing to worry about.

Enzymes

These are natural proteins which are found in all living things, animal and vegetable. Enzymes are catalysts which trigger change such as deterioration for example fruit and vegetable discolouration.

Enzymes are most active at temperatures between 29°C and 50°C however they are fragile and can easily be destroyed through exposure to high temperatures over 60°C or slowed down by cold exposure

Bacteria

Bacteria are not visible to the human eye and they multiply rapidly at temperatures between 20°C and 40°C, but are destroyed at temperatures over 60°C. They cannot be destroyed through freezing, instead they just lie dormant. Bacteria cause food to deteriorate and some bacteria causes' food poisoning, so it is vital that these are destroyed during the preserving process.

Mould

Mould thrives in warm and humid conditions and is a form of microscopic fungi. Mould spores will settle on any fruit and vegetables and start to form a greenish grey powdery appearance on the surface. The spores that give the greenish grey colour to mould are released when dry so that they can become airborne and spread to create new moulds. Some moulds are friendly for example in the production of hard-rind cheeses, but many will cause decay and can be toxic.

Mould thrives at temperatures between 10°C and 38°c but can be destroyed at temperatures between 60-90°C

Yeast

Yeast is part of the fungi group of organisms and when found in food is generally not harmful to our health but it can cause food to spoil. Most yeast will grow in food containing over 60% sugar if it is badly covered allowing air to get to it but it can be destroyed at temperatures above 60°C

Four Steps for Excluding Spoilers from Your Preserves:

1. Hygiene: all equipment and work surfaces need to be thoroughly cleaned and sanitised.
2. Sterilisation: All jars or bottles to be used for your finished preserves must be sterilised thoroughly prior to use.
3. The high concentrations of sugar, acidity, alcohol or salt in preserve mixtures serve to kill off the spoilers.
4. Abide by heating guidelines to ensure that spoilers are destroyed.
5. The final step is excluding air from the finished product. Ensure that all jars are sealed tightly and cleanly to prevent bacteria and exclude air. The golden rule is work quickly and cleanly.

Storage

Pickles, chutneys, jams and other preserves should be stored in a cool, dry, dark, airy place where the temperature variation is minimal. Hot and steamy kitchens are far from ideal for storing preserves, but if there is no alternative then choose shelves that are near to the floor. This will be a cooler area than higher up and hopefully below the reach of the hot air, steam and condensation that rises from cooking practices. The ideal storage conditions for keeping preserves are a steady, low temperature that is not damp. Warm and damp environments are not suitable for keeping any preserves and should be avoided.

The Preserving Year

The busiest time in the preserving year is in the late summer and early autumn when the hedgerows will be heavy with fruit, groaning to be picked and everywhere, produce is in abundance. However, if the mood takes you your preserving pan can be bubbling for three hundred and sixty five days of the year for at any given time some crop will be in season.

Seasonality Chart

Use the seasonality charts to plan your preserving year

Pectin

Pectin is a naturally occurring thickening agent found mostly in the skin and core of fruit, when combined with acid and sugar it forms a gel, the essential process for setting jams and marmalades. The level of set achieved in your preserve is going to be affected by the type of fruit in the recipe and the natural pectin levels of that fruit. Although setting of low pectin fruits can be aided by the addition of pectin rich fruits, home-made pectin stock, commercial liquid pectin, powdered pectin or lemon juice.

What's in Season?

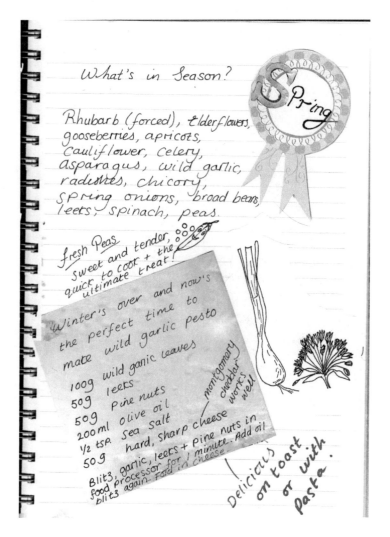

Spring

Rhubarb (forced), Elderflowers, gooseberries, apricots, cauliflower, celery, asparagus, wild garlic, radishes, chicory, spring onions, broad beans, leeks, spinach, peas.

Fresh Peas
Sweet and tender, quick to cook + the ultimate treat!

Winter's over and now's the perfect time to make wild garlic pesto

- 100g wild garlic leaves
- 50g leeks
- 50g pine nuts
- 200ml olive oil
- 1/2 tsp sea salt
- 50g hard, sharp cheese

Montgomery 'cheddar' works well

Blitz garlic, leeks + pine nuts in food processor for 1 minute. Add oil, blitz again. Fold in cheese.

Delicious on toast or with pasta.

Summer

What's in season?

Strawberries, cherries, blackcurrant, peach, plums, blackberries, rhubarb, gooseberries, raspberries, grapes, pears, greengages, elderflowers, apricots, redcurrants, blueberries, bilberries, figs, damsons, broad beans, courgettes, radishes, runner beans, peppers, cucumbers, asparagus, peas, fennel, sweetcorn, tomatoes, spring-onion.

Strawberry Jam

1.4 kg strawberries,
900g sugar
150 ml water
big slice of lemon

Hull and rinse the straw-
berries. Place in the
preserving pan with the
sugar, water and lemon.
Simmer until the sugar
dissolves. Bring to the
boil & boil rapidly for 10 mins.
Stir occasionally - check for set.

always pick fruit on dry, sunny days!

* Don't forget to pick the elderflowers before they smell can!

- 14 -

autumn

What's in Season?

apples, blueberries, blackberries, Victoria plums, cranberries, quince, elderberries, figs, pears, carrots, celeriac, celery, pumpkin, courgette, parsnips, tomatoes, peppers, radishes, onions, turnips.

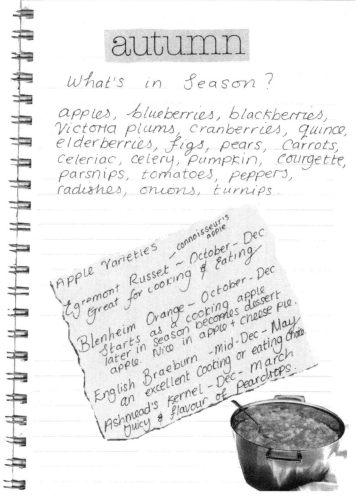

Apple Varieties

Egremont Russet - connoisseur's apple
October - Dec
Great for cooking & eating

Blenheim Orange - October - Dec
Starts as a cooking apple
later in season becomes dessert
apple. Nice in apple + cheese pie.

English Braeburn - Mid-Dec - May
an excellent cooking or eating choice.

Ashmead's kernel - Dec - march
Juicy & flavour of pear drops.

What's in Season?

Seville oranges, pomegranate, clementine, blood oranges, cranberries, rhubarb (forced), leeks, artichokes, brussel sprouts, celery, cabbage, parsnips.

When is the Best time of year to make marmalade? **NOW!**

SHORT SEASON

The Seville orange season starts in mid December and ends in Jan/Feb

pips contain more Pectin + requires less sugar to get its consistency = tangy + delicious!

The Bitter orange

Winter
Pomegranate,
blood orang
rhubarb (for
artichokes,
celery, cabba

Guide to the Pectin Content of Key Fruit

high	medium	low
Apples (cooking)	Apples (desert)	Blackberries (late)
Apples (crab)	Blackberries (early)	Elderberries
Citrus Fruit	Blueberries	Figs
Currents (red, black, white)	Greengages	Peaches
Damsons	Mulberries	Pears
Gooseberries	Raspberries(ripe & unripe) Sloes	Plums (sweet)
Plums (sour)	Fresh apricots	Strawberries
Quince		Cherries
Cranberries		Medlars
Grapes		Marrow
		Mulberries
		rhubarb

Making Home-Made Pectin Stock

There are lots of commercial pectin brands readily available in both liquid and powder form and these are labour saving and reliable, but if you want to be economical and have a glut of apples then making home-made pectin stock may be the ideal solution.

Homemade pectin can be made in the early summer if you have direct access to apple trees or in autumn when apples are in season.

You will need small, green, immature apples: wild crab apples are a great source of pectin, but any immature apple will do. You may use damaged apples, but you will need to cut away all the imperfections first. Under no circumstances throw imperfect apples into the pan as it will lead to spoilage.

Ingredients

900g Tart green apples
2 unwaxed lemons (seeded)
940 ml water

Method

Chop the lemons, reserving the peel and pips. The Rinds and pips are where all the pectin is.

Wash the apples, trim and discard any bruised or damaged parts and slice them very thinly, retaining pips, skins and cores. Place them in a heavy bottomed (non-reactive) pan with the chopped up lemons, and add the water.

Over a high heat, bring the mixture to a rolling boil stirring constantly. Reduce the heat and simmer for 20 minutes or until the fruit is tender and pulpy. Continue to stir occasionally so the fruit does not stick to the pan and singe.

Remove from the heat and cool. Line a bowl large enough to hold the liquid with dampened cheesecloth/muslin. Pour the pulp and juice into the cheesecloth/ muslin. Gather the corners and tie in a knot. Carefully lift over the bowl. Suspend from a cupboard handle or hook and allow to drip into the bowl overnight. Resist all temptation - do not stir the liquid and do not squeeze the bag.

The next day, measure the juice and pour into a large pan. Discard the contents of the cheesecloth. Bring the liquid rapidly to the boil, stirring constantly, reduce the heat, and cook over a low heat until reduced by half.

The pectin needs to be stored in sterilised jam jars with 2cm headroom. Once in jars the pectin needs to be processed in a boiling water bath for 5 minutes.

Using Homemade Pectin

When using homemade pectin, you can't follow the recipes that are found on the backs of commercially available pectin bottles. With homemade pectin you will need to use equal amounts of pectin to low pectin fruits: for example 900g strawberries to 900ml homemade pectin. With all fruits that are low in pectin including: blueberries, cherries, peaches, raspberries, rhubarb and strawberries, follow the equal quantities rule.

With high pectin fruits such as apples, cranberries, quinces, currants and plums, cut the quantity of homemade pectin in half.

Acidity in Fruit

The natural acid in fruit helps to release its pectin stores and avoids the need for lengthy cooking.

Key Fruit Acidity Chart:

High Acidity	Medium Acidity	Low Acidity
Blackcurrants	Quinces	Medlars
Crab apples	Apricots	Blackberries
Gooseberries	Cooking apples	Figs
Damsons	Ripe plums	Pears
Unripe plums	Raspberries	Strawberries
Greengages	Mulberries	Cherries
Citrus Fruits	Grapes	Blueberries
Rhubarb	Sloes	Peaches
	Cranberries	

If the acid levels of a chosen fruit is low then to improve its colour, taste and setting properties the acid level will need to be raised and this can be done by adding tartaric acid, citric acid or the juice of one lemon to every 1kg of fruit you use.

Tartaric Acid

This is a naturally occurring acid in plants and is found in high volume in sour fruits. It can be purchased in a powdered form and is used to aid the setting of jams. Check the instructions on the pack, but generally 1tsp. of tartaric acid per 900g of fruit used, is mixed with a little water and added to the jam pan at the end of the cooking process.

Citric Acid

Citric acid is found naturally in the juice of lemons and other citrus fruits. It strengthens the set in jams by controlling the PH level and also adds tartness to the flavour. It is readily available from chemists and specialist baking supplies as a crystalline powder.

Choosing Ingredients:

Sugars

Ordinary granulated sugar is the cheapest to buy and unless a recipe states otherwise this is the one to opt for. Some people like to warm the sugar before adding it to jam recipes to reduce the risk of crystallisation; I have rarely found this necessary, but some recipes require this step.

Special preserving sugar which contains pectin can be purchased to ensure a set is achieved in jams, but it is more expensive and with a bit of care and practice a good set can be achieved without using it.

Brown sugars are used mainly in marmalades and chutneys where its colour will not adversely affect the appearance of the preserve.

Salts

Generally rock salt should be used in preserving to achieve the best results. Sea salt has a high content of iodine which can cause problems with preserves and the additives used in table salt to prevent it clumping can make preserves cloudy.

Vinegar

Malt vinegar is by far the cheapest option, but it has a strong flavour and colour. The white distilled vinegar has the advantage of not imparting colour. For delicate pickles and chutneys wine vinegars are ideal. Wine vinegars give a more subtle flavour and are good for pickling spiced fruits such as plums and damsons. Using cider vinegar will boost the colour and flavour in fruity chutneys. Using cider or wine vinegars will also reduce the time chutneys need to mature.

Making your own fruit, herb or spice vinegars can add some interesting flavours to your pickles, chutneys and dressings. To make raspberry or blackberry vinegar put 450g/1lb of fresh raspberries or blackberries into 600ml/20fl oz. of white wine vinegar and leave for a week before straining through muslin and pouring into sterilised bottles. Or make herb vinegar, by substituting the fruit for 25g/1oz of fresh tarragon, sage, rosemary or mint.

Any preserve made with vinegar needs to be given time to mature. Chutneys need to be left for a few weeks, when using wine vinegar and a few months if malt vinegar has been used, to allow the flavours to mellow. Vegetable and fruit pickles contain larger amounts of vinegar and less sugar and so need 3-6 weeks before they are ready.

Whatever, vinegar you choose it needs to be good quality with an acetic acid content of 5% minimum otherwise your preserves will not keep as well.

Equipment

We don't have to regress very far into our culinary history to come across preserved foods. There was a time when preserving was an essential skill and whether you were a pauper or a king preserved food would be a mainstay of your diet. Before the advent of modern glass jam jars with their neat little screw top lids, bullock's bladders would be washed and soaked in warm water to make them pliable before being stretched across the top of stone preserving jars and tied down with string to create a seal for the jar. Another widely used method was to pour a little melted mutton fat on top of the preserves which when set would create an effective air excluding layer. Today there is an array of modern, reliable equipment readily available, but many of the recipes in this book can be tackled with only basic equipment, much of which you may already have in your kitchen cupboards.

The list of equipment is not exhaustive, meaning that you will be able to make a start on preserving without making an expensive outlay.

What you will need:

Large saucepan and preserving pan (Maslin pan)
Measuring jug
Oven gloves
Selection of clean cotton tea towels
Kitchen scales
Wooden spoons
Ladle
Sharp knives

Pyrex or ceramic kitchen bowls
Muslin
Jam jars
Labels
Lemon juicer
Potato masher

Useful Equipment:

These things you may already have, but if you do have to acquire them they should not prove too expensive. This equipment is not essential for getting started, but as your preserving repertoire grows your equipment range will need to become more comprehensive.

Mincer
Grater
Sieves
Jam tongs
Large preserving jars
Strainer
Jam funnel
Preserving thermometer
Jelly bag
Slotted spoon
Colander

If you acquire all the equipment in both lists you should be able to tackle most preserving recipes you come across.

Kitchen Bowls: made of heat proof glass, Pyrex or ceramic. Look around for really large ones for the times when you want to make a huge batch of something.

Measuring Jug: A standard heat-proof, one pint measuring jug

Wooden Spoons: An array of different wooden spoons is always useful, but you will need a few with extra-long handles, for the times when continuous stirring is required and you need to keep your distance from the heat.

Scales: Just a set that work accurately

Sharp Knives: You only really need two good, sharp knives. A general purpose knife with a blade around 12cm long and a longer bladed chopping knife of approx. 25cm.

Muslin: Mainly used for straining.

Jelly Bag: Good kitchen supply shops will sell these for straining jellies and syrups. You can manage with muslin cloth, but a jelly bag makes life easier.

Grater: Any good grater will do, this is mainly used for grating citrus zest.

Juicer: for juicing lemons and other citrus fruits

Mincer: For mincing up ingredients. The old-fashioned ones are great and very robust, providing you have a surface to bolt them on to.

Labels: Nothing fancy is required, just something that adheres to the jar well; otherwise you will spend time pondering over the mysterious contents of your jars.

Slotted Spoon: Basically a serving spoon with holes in it.

Masher: A potato masher is often useful when needing to crush soft fruits.

Ladle: A small ladle is useful for decanting preserves into sterilised jam jars.

Funnels: specialist jam funnels are available, but if you don't have one, a large plastic one for general use will be fine.

Sieves and Strainers: These should be nylon and the finer the mesh the better.

Colander: a large colander is always useful when straining and washing vegetables

Saucepans: thick bottomed pans are preferable to prevent burning

Thermometer: a preserving thermometer is not essential in home preserving, but it does make things easier some times, especially if you are struggling to find setting points.

Preserving/Maslin Pan: if you are buying one new, go for the largest size you can afford as it will give you the flexibility of bigger batch sizes.

Jam tongs: not essential, but handy when getting hot jars out of pans full of boiling water.

Tea Towels: A selection of clean cotton tea towels is always handy when preserving

Oven Gloves: For getting hot jars out of the oven etc.

Chapter Two
Jammy Devil: The Alchemy of Jam Making

Grab your best pinny and prepare to get sticky, it's time to make jam!

Making jam and preserves has seen resurgence in popularity, once seen as old fashioned and only for members of the Women's Institute or those women with nothing better to do, now it has never been so popular and is suddenly seen as hot and trendy. Its new found popularity is well deserved for there is nothing on earth more sumptuous than a dollop of glossy, sticky, fruit packed, oozing jam.

Whether you call it 'conserve', 'preserve' or simply 'jam', no afternoon tea, scone, Victoria sponge or summer afternoon would be complete without it. The precise origin of jam remains a matter of historical debate; however, one thing that every food historian can agree on is that jams have a rich history and are appreciated worldwide for their taste, texture and rich and sumptuous aroma.

What is agreed about jam history is that it appears in the very first known recipe, "Of Culinary Matters", penned by the great Roman gastronome Marcus Gavius Apicius in the first century AD. It's thought to have taken off in Europe following the Spanish arrival in the West Indies, where fruit preservation was well established. Jams remained an aristocratic luxury for most of the remainder of the millennium, with Louis XIV a particular fan: he insisted that all banquets ended with fruit preserves served in silver dishes. Jams made their way to England in the Tudor period, with quince and medlar being regularly incorporated in recipes.

If you have never made jam then it is difficult to explain how such a simple and methodical art can give rise to such bliss. Indeed there is much pleasure to be gained from jam making, it is a gently chaotic art that fills the air with the smells of summer gluttony and lifts the spirits on the dullest of days. The perpetual stirring of plump; ripe fruit and melting sugar; the meticulous preparation of jars and pans; the transformation of ingredients into sticky brilliance; the art of neatly filling warm jars with gluttonous, indulgent, gleaming, sweet jam.

The feeling of accomplishment as you stare quietly awe stricken by the beauty of neatly labeled rows of jam and the realisation that you are a very grown-up cook that has discovered the secrets of kitchen alchemy.

Whilst jam is made in order to preserve a glut of fruit or to help get you through the long and dismal days of winter, practicality aside making jam, makes your life feel like it is in order; it restores faith in your own ability and makes you feel that there is hope when everything appears hopeless, giving you inequitable assurance that you are one of life's great achievers.

Setting aside the great pleasures that can be derived from making your own jam, there is a very good argument for home-made jam revolving around taste. It could be argued that if you've never tasted home-made jam then you have never tasted jam, for nowadays, commercial jam has become one of those products which has suffered at the hands of mass production. The food industry's insistence that customers want only the cheapest food has led to the proliferation of cheap, sugary jams that have the consistency of rubber balls and tractor tyres. You can help to re-establish the value of jam by making your own delicious, fruit packed jam at home.

If you don't go in for sentiment and nostalgia then approach jam making for the sake of frugality for during the summer and early autumn, fresh produce is abundant, which makes jam making excellent value. Whether you want to follow the latest craze for foraging and pick your blackberries and crab apples for free or you prefer to buy more exotic fruits; the pleasure of jam making is boundless and by far the best therapy for any cook, stressed parent or those with a weary heart. The world can feel a much better place when immersed in the sweet smell of soft simmering fruit and melting sugar.

Only the Finest Ingredients are allowed:

Use only fruit that is in good and edible condition; discard any fruit that is moldy, bruised over-ripe or has gone bad, the basic rule is if you wouldn't eat it raw, then don't put it your jam. Only fruit in top condition will give your precious jam that fresh, fruity aroma and tempting jewel like colours.

Covering and Bottling Jam:

It is absolutely essential that you prepare your jars correctly if the jam is to keep. You can either warm the thoroughly washed jars in a cooling oven, thereby sterilising them, or you can immerse them in boiling water for 10 minutes or run them through the hottest cycle of the dishwasher.

Whichever sterilising method is employed the storage jars must be clean and hot when you pour the hot jam into them. Use a small, sterilised jug for pouring jam into jars, this will help to minimise mess and maximise speed. Remember, success in keeping jam depends on the speedy exclusion of air, so work quickly, cleanly and make sure that the jars are sealed well.

Seal the jars with a disc of waxed or greaseproof paper that you have cut earlier. The transparent jam covers that can be bought in kitchenware shops and supermarkets should be applied whilst the jam is still warm so that they shrink over the top of the jar and create an air-tight seal.

Achieving a Good Set:

If you want a fool proof way of ensuring that the setting point has been reached, then invest in a jam thermometer. Using a thermometer: Jams and marmalade's reach a setting point once they have been boiled at 105C / 220F for 10 to 15 minutes.

For the traditionalists which includes myself, simply chill two saucers in the freezer, removing them when you think your jam has reached setting point and then place a spoonful on one of the cold plates, leave it for a couple of minutes, and then the jam should wrinkle when you push it with your finger. If it doesn't pass the wrinkle test, simply boil a little longer and try again with the second chilled plate.

However, once you have made a few batches of jam you will begin to notice that a good indication of the jam having reached setting point is that the rapid frothing ceases and the jam makes fabulous heavy, thud like plopping noises. Always, turn the heat off before doing any setting test otherwise you may be over boiling the jam whilst testing it.

A knob of Butter

A knob of butter added just before the end of the cooking process gives jam a really nice glossy shine. It also serves to make the scum easier to remove as it collects it in one place. After finishing the cooking process lift the scum off with a metal spoon and discard.

A drop of Glycerine

Pure glycerine stirred in 2 minutes before the jam is ready to be potted up, will increase its preserving qualities. Use 1tsp. glycerine to every 1.8kg of jam.

Traits of a Good Jam

You know you've made a good jam if it is firm without being solid, clear, bright, and glossy and with a good flavour. Simple Strawberry Jam is perfect for slathering over fresh white bread. Strawberry jam is a childhood favourite and the best friend of the scone, who let's face it without a generous filling of red gorgeousness is not a true treat. The homemade version of this British classic is infinitely better than anything you can buy in the shops; less sugary, more defined, more fruity, and above all, softer and stickier with good old-fashioned nostalgia. I must admit I like to wallow in the joy of jam making, it is one of those activities that in such a fast paced world seems like a luxury to indulge in. The biggest challenge in making strawberry jam is achieving a good set. The principle problem to overcome when making strawberry jam is their lack of pectin. The more acidic the fruit, the more pectin it is likely to contain, so the intense sweetness of the fully ripe and oh so deliciously oozy strawberry is not helpful on the setting front.

Fear not: there are three ways to up the pectin quota: firstly, with the juice of a more acidic fruit, such as lemon, secondly by using jam sugar (which includes pectin),but I personally dislike for I feel it achieves too firmer set and thirdly by adding some pectin in liquid form to ordinary sugar although this not the route for the jam purists.

Ingredients:

3tbsp lemon juice,
900g fruit strawberries prepared weight
900g golden granulated sugar
knob of butter

Method:

Place the prepared fruit in preserving pan or large heavy-based saucepan. Add 150 ml of water and 3tbsp lemon juice. Bring to the boil and then reduce to a nice simmer for five minutes after which the fruit should be plump and soft. Add in the sugar and stir over a very low heat until the sugar has completely dissolved. Raise the heat and bring to a full rolling boil, then rapidly boil the strawberries for 20-25 minutes, until the setting point of 105C is reached. Remove from the heat; skim off any excess scum, then stir a knob of butter across the surface. Leave for about 15 mins, so the fruit can settle and prevent the fruit in the jam sinking to the bottle. Pour the warm jam into sterilised jars, label and seal.

Simple Apple Jam

A great way of using up a glut of cooking apples, this recipe is simple to master and the results are a fantastic way to spice up a cheese sandwich, but it's also a great addition to cooking sauces, stews and casseroles. This recipe is also low on preparation work, so it's a nice recipe to do when you are not relishing the thought of laborious kitchen labour.

Ingredients:

2.7 kg (tart) cooking apples
2.2 kg sugar
1.1 litres of water
3 lemons (juice and rind only)
5 cloves
1 cinnamon stick

Method:

Wash the apples, remove the stalks, and slice coarsely without peeling or coring. Put into a preserving pan with the lemon juice and lemon rind. Place the cloves and cinnamon stick in a piece of muslin and tie it to the pan handle. Add the water and cook until the apples are very tender and reduced to a pulp. Rub through a sieve. Put the sieved pulp back into the cleaned preserving pan and add the sugar. Bring to the boil slowly, and then simmer rapidly for 10 minutes. Test for setting on a cold plate or else use your jam thermometer. When the apple jam reaches setting point, pot immediately into hot sterilised jars, seal and label.

Apple and Ginger Jam

A real pick-me-up in the morning when spread over toast or spooned into creamy porridge. No cold morning should be faced without a jar of Apple and Ginger jam in store and no winter rice pudding can quite hit the spot without a generous dollop of thick, sumptuous jam.

Ingredients:

3kg cooking (tart) apples
1.2 litres water
Grated rind and juice of 4 lemons
50g fresh ginger (bruised)
3kg granulated sugar

Method:

Peel, core and chop the apples. Reserve the peelings and core and tie in a muslin bag and put with the apple and water into the preserving pan. Add the finely grated lemon rind and the juice, together with the ginger. Simmer for 20 minutes or until pulpy, then squeeze out the peeling bag to release all the pectin and discard. Remove the piece of fresh ginger and discard. Stir in the sugar and boil until setting point is reached. Remove from the heat, skim, pot, cover, and label.

Marrow and Ginger Jam

A traditional way to use up marrows that are either in abundance on the allotment or have grown too big to prove tasty in other recipes. This jam is surprisingly sweet and delicious on fresh bread.

Ingredients:

1.5kg marrow
1.5kg sugar
2 lemons (rind and juice)
25g bruised root ginger

Method:

Prepare the marrow by peeling, removing the seeds and cutting into cubes. Alternate layers of marrow and sugar in an earthenware bowl and leave in a cool place overnight. The next day peel the rind of the lemons (without the pith) and tie them in a muslin bag along with the bruised root ginger. Place the marrow and its juices in a preserving pan along with the muslin bag and slowly bring to the boil. Whilst waiting for the marrow to come to the boil, juice the lemons and add to the boiling pan along with the sugar. When the sugar has dissolved, continue to gently simmer until the marrow looks transparent and the syrup is thick. Stir occasionally to stop the jam from sticking to the bottom of the pan. Remove the muslin bag and pour into warm and sterilised jars and cover.

Storecupboard Dried Fruit Jam

There are times when the urge to make jam is strong, but you have no fresh ingredients in store, this recipe for dried fruit jam is delicious and a good way to use up all those bits of dried fruit left over from Christmas cake making.

Ingredients:

500g mixed dried fruit (apples, pears, apricots, plums, prunes or whatever you have)
1.2 litres water
1kg sugar (warm in the oven before use)
1 orange
1 lemon

Method:

Place the dried fruit in an earthenware bowl with the water and leave covered in a cool place overnight. The next day remove any stones from the fruit and place the fruit and its liquor into a preserving pan. Grate the rinds of the orange and lemon and squeeze out the juice, adding to the pan. Bring the contents of the pan to the boil and then reduce the heat to a happy simmer for around an hour by this time the fruits should be very soft. Add the warmed sugar and stir over a very low heat until the sugar has completely dissolved. Bring to a rapid boil until setting point is reached. Remove any scum and cool for 10 minutes before potting, to avoid the fruit sinking.

Raspberry Jam

On those bright summer days it's easy to forget those dreary winter days when you need a generous helping of jam on your scone just to perk you up. Good raspberry jam can help dispel those winter blues with a taste of summer.

Ingredients:

1.5kg raspberries
1.5kg sugar

Method:

Place the raspberries into a preserving pan and set of a gentle heat, stirring occasionally until they begin to boil. Stir in the sugar and stir continuously until the sugar has completely dissolved. Bring the mixture to a full, rolling boil for five minutes. Check for the setting point and once reached bottle in warm jars and seal.

Gooseberry Jam

Gooseberries see a short season in the midst of summer - between June and July, but their sharp and zingy flavour can be savoured all year round with this lovely jam recipe.

Ingredients:

1.5 kg gooseberries
2kg sugar
600ml water

Method:

Top and tail the gooseberries, wash and drain them. Place the prepared fruit into a preserving pan with the water and cook gently until deliciously soft and pulpy. Add the sugar and stir until completely dissolved and then bring to a rapid boil until the setting point is reached. This should take around 15-20 minutes. Ladle into sterilised jars whilst still warm.

Greengage Jam

A classic British fruit, greengages are sweet and immensely pleasing when ripe. They make deeply delicious jam that is ideal for filling sponge sandwich cakes.

Ingredients

2kg Ripe Greengages,
1.5 kg sugar.

Method:

Remove the stones from the ripe fruit. Retain the stones.

Place the fruit in the preserving pan with half of the sugar and allow to stand for several hours.

Meanwhile, blanch the stones in boiling water for three minutes. Drain them and then crack half of the stones open and remove the kernels. Add the kernels to the fruit mixture.

Now place the pan on a medium heat and allow the fruit to simmer until it is soft and pulpy. Now add the rest of the sugar simmer whilst stirring until the sugar has dissolved. Bring to the boil for 30-40 minutes (stirring occasionally) and test for setting point. Pour the jam into warm pots and seal.

Take your Bletted Medlars....

The small rusty brown fruit known as the medlar was a favourite of both the Greeks and the Romans, but it was the Elizabethans and Victorians who were the real fans this peculiar looking fruit.

In Shakespeare's England bletted medlars would have been as commonplace as ripened pears. In Shakespeare's "Romeo and Juliet", Mercutio makes reference to the wonderful medlar,

"Now will he sit under a medlar tree,
And wish his mistress were that kind of fruit
As maids call medlars, when they laugh alone.
O Romeo, that she were, O that she were
An open-arse and thou a poperin pear!"

Now there is sexual euphemism galore about these lines, with the long tapering poperin pear being bardly slang for penis, but due to the appearance of the Medlar fruit with its retained sepals and hollow crowned appearance has itself been long been used euphemistically by the English to refer to the anus ("open-arse"), less commonly female genitalia ("open tail") or the endearing term of "dog's arse". Now this may all seem very earthy, but when you take a look at this little fruit it all makes sense.

Completely inedible until it has begun to rot, the medlar has been the subject of many a strange description and definition including this one from the The Complete Dictionary of the Vulgar Tongue, published in 1811:

"A fruit, vulgarly called an open arse; of which it is more truly than delicately said, that it is never ripe till it is as rotten as a turd, and then it is not worth a fart."

The rotting process called "bletting" that medlar fruits must be subjected to before being used in recipes can occur while the fruit is still attached to the tree. Simply leave the fruit on the tree and harvest after the first frost blackens the fruit. Alternatively, harvest the fruit as soon as there is a slight softening of the flesh and store it in a cool place for around three weeks. The flesh will change from cream to dark purple and will have a smell of fermenting fruit about it.

Medlar Jam

This wonderful sweet and sharp, glossy jam is an historical gem that is well worth re-creating.

Ingredients:

1.5 kg ripe Medlars, (bletted)
1.1 kg sugar,
3 lemons, juice and grated rind (zest),
600ml water

Method:

Place some soft ripe medlars in a preserving pan, and add just enough water to cover them. Allow to simmer, stirring gently every few minutes. After half an hour of simmering the medlars will begin to split. Pass the fruit through a coarse sieve back into a clean pan. Add the grated rind (zest) and the juice of the lemons and the sugar to the sieved fruit. Bring to a rapid boil until the jam sets when tested. Pour into warm jars and sealed.

Credit to Layla Long

Banana Jam

This rich and flavoursome jam is ideal spooned into porridge, great in cakes and makes a nice change in a rice pudding. Of course you might like to just spread it on your toast for breakfast.

Ingredients:

2.8 kg bananas (peeled weight)
1 kg pears,
two lemons,
2.3 kg sugar.
Knob of butter (optional)

Method:

Peel and slice the bananas and check the peeled weight. Pare and dice the pears. Place 500g of the sugar, the juice of two lemons, and the pears into a preserving-pan, and simmer until soft. Add the remaining sugar and stir until dissolved. Now add the banana, stirring carefully. Add a knob of butter and continue to stir. Increase the heat and bring the mixture to the boil for forty minutes. Allow to cool slightly and skim before ladling into warm jars and sealing.

Elderberry Jam

Elderberries can be picked in late autumn and have anti-viral qualities, so are ideal to include in winter jam. The taste of the fruit alone is slightly earthy with bitter edge which benefits from the addition of the orange flower water.

Ingredients

2.75 kg ripe elderberries
1.5 kg sugar
1 tbsp. orange flower water
600ml water

Method:

Remove the stalks from the elderberries and place them in a preserving-pan with barely enough water to cover the fruit. Bring to the boil and then reduce the heat and simmer for twenty minutes. Add the sugar and orange-flower water and stir until dissolved. Bring to the boil and stir occasionally for forty-five minutes. Check for the setting point and skim before potting.

Quince Jam.

A glorious rich coloured jam that varies from tones of ruby red to bright coral. The quince is highly fragranced when ripe and has a slightly floral flavour that it imparts in this special jam.

Ingredients

2 kg quinces
Water
Sugar
Juice of two lemons

Method:

Peel and dice the quinces into small cubes, place into a preserving pan and cover with water. Simmer for between 30-45 minutes or until soft and pulpy. Next measure the pulp and to every 600ml of pulp add 500g of sugar. Return the pulp with the sugar to the pan and stir thoroughly. Add the lemon juice and set over a moderate heat, stirring continuously until the sugar has dissolved. Bring to the boil and maintain a rapid boil for around twenty minutes, then test for the setting point. Pour into warm jars and seal.

Pear Jam.

This is not a quick jam to make, but it's well worth the effort, beautifully rich and warming, it's ideal for slathering on toast.

Ingredients

1.8 kg firm pears
1.4 kg of sugar
60g of grated ginger root.
Grated Zest and Juice of two lemons

Method

Slice the fruit very thinly and place in a preserving-pan, with the grated ginger, lemon zest and lemon juice. Bring the mixture gradually to the boil, and then reduce to a slow simmer for three hours, or until it is quite thick and clear. Ladle into warm jars and seal

Rhubarb Jam

This wonderfully rosy rhubarb jam. The warming additions of candied peel and ginger makes a rather decadent breakfast jam, ideal for those mornings when you need to take off the chill and indulge yourself.

Ingredients:

3.6 kg rhubarb,
3.6 kg sugar,
25 g grated ginger,
500g of chopped candied peel.

Method:

Clean the rhubarb and cut it into pieces about one inch (2.5cm) long. Place the fruit in a pan, spread the sugar over the rhubarb and cover the pan. Leave it until the next day and then add the ginger and candied peel and boil for 1-1 ½ hours, by which time it will turn a rich red colour. Pour it into sterilised jars and seal it at once.

Mulberry Jam.

A dazzlingly red jam that is sweet and intense. If you are lucky enough to have mulberries to hand this is a jam well worth making.

Ingredients:

1kg Mulberries
1 kg sugar

Method:

Take ripe mulberries and let them simmer in their own juice till they are tender but not broken. Then add the sugar and stir until dissolved. Bring to the boil and rapidly boil until the setting point is reached. (around 20 minutes). Ladle into warm jars and seal.

Jam for Instant Gratification

These jams won't keep for a long time, but in this lies part of their appeal. These jams are for immediate eating, for the instant sweet fix and for devouring in great gluttonous dollops without consideration for tomorrow. No they are not for the jam purist, but they are for the desperate foodie that just longs to eat warm jam, fresh out of the pan.

Sticky Salted Caramel Apple Jam

This juicy apple jam is swirled with sticky toffee sauce, perfect for spreading on hot toast, swirling through thick custard and dolloping on scones or just eating off the spoon should the mood take you.

Ingredients:

600g cooking apples (cored and peeled weight)
100ml water
1 vanilla pod (split)
2 tbsp. lemon juice
250g white granulated sugar
For the Salted Caramel sauce
100g light muscovado sugar
4 tbsp. golden syrup
100g unsalted butter
1tsp fine sea salt
4 tbsp. double cream

Method:

First make the toffee sauce. Melt the sugar, syrup and butter in a small, heavy bottomed pan and bring slowly to the boil. Reduce the heat and simmer gently for a few minutes, until thick. Remove from the heat and stir in the cream, add the salt, stir thoroughly, set aside to cool.

To make the apple jam. Place the apples, water, vanilla pods and lemon juice in a pan and cook gently until soft and mushy, this will take about 15-20 minutes. Once the apples have become soft and squidgy, add the sugar and cook over a low heat, stirring until all the sugar has dissolved. Now turn up the heat and bring to a rolling boil for approximately five minutes. The apple jam should be thick and sticky. Take your pre-prepared jar and add a layer of toffee sauce to the bottom followed by a layer of apple jam and continue layering until you reach the top of the jar. Now you have beautiful stripey jar of moreish, gooey, sticky Salted Caramel Apple Jam.

You can store the jam in the fridge and eat within 4 weeks. Once opened it will need to be eaten within 3 days although eating this scrumptious jam is never an issue.

Here and Now Rhubarb Jam

Rhubarb jam; pure, simple and a quintessential reminder of all things great and British. This jam is an absolute must swirled into rich, creamy rice pudding or dolloped onto sponge puds. This jam will thicken further once cooled but it is a soft set, indulgent type of jam that is designed for eating not keeping.

Ingredients:

1.2kg fresh rhubarb, chopped
400g caster sugar
2 teaspoons grated orange zest
80ml orange juice
125ml water

Method:

In a heavy bottomed saucepan or preserving pan, combine the rhubarb, sugar, orange zest, orange juice and water. Bring to the boil, and then cook over low heat for 45 minutes, stirring occasionally until thick and mushy. Ladle into hot sterile jars and once cool store in the refrigerator.

When Things Don't Go According to Plan

A Crust of Mould Forming

If mould starts to grow on top of home-made jam, it doesn't spell the end of the jar of jam, spoon it off and hope for the best. Mould forms on the top of jam for one of three reasons either the jars are not properly sterilised; the fruit was picked while wet or the jam has not been stored properly.

The next time you make preserves take extra care to ensure the thorough sterilisation of jars and lids. When applying lids make sure a good airtight seal has formed to exclude air. When you store your preserves make sure you find a cool, dark and dry place as warm and damp conditions can encourage the growth of mould.

Crystallisation

Sugar crystals appear on top and sometimes through the jam. The jam is safe to eat but will taste very sweet with an uneven texture

Crystallisation is caused when:

(a)   Too much sugar is added
(b)   The sugar is not properly dissolved
(c)   The jam is over- or under-boiled

For future batches take care to weigh the sugar out and ensure that the sugar is fully dissolved before bringing to the boil.

Fermentation

When fermentation occurs, the jam will start to bubble and can smell gassy when the lid is removed. This is a sign that yeast is present and is reacting with the sugar. Jam that has fermented should be discarded; it is not fit for eating. Fermentation can occur when:

(a)   The jam is undercooked
(b)   The fruit was wet when harvested
(c)   The jars were not properly cleaned and sterilised

The fruit has floated to the top of your preserve

This is a learning curve as there is nothing that can be done after the preserve has been potted and sealed, but to avoid this happening to future batches let your preserve rest for 10 minutes once setting point has been reached. This will allow you to see if the fruit rises to the top, if it does stir the preserve to redistribute the fruit and then pot immediately.

Poor Set

The most common problem when it comes to preserve making is achieving a good set. A poor set can occur for a number of reasons;

1. too much or too little sugar was used
2. an insufficient amount of pectin may have been used,
3. the fruit used was either over ripe or under ripe
4. You may have cooked your mixture for too long.

The good news is that setting problems can be rectified. Simply follow the steps below and with 'a bit of luck and a little black pig' as the saying goes you will end up with a perfectly set preserve.

Step one: sterilise a new set of jars

Step two: empty the runny preserve back into your jam pan and bring it back to the boil whilst stirring it constantly to stop it from sticking, allow it to boil for 1 minute then re-test the set. If the set is now correct then re-pot and seal your jars. Job done!

However, if the set is still runny then you must try adding pectin. I recommend commercial liquid pectin for this job and you will need approximately half the amount of pectin that is indicated by your original recipe.

Exercise caution when adding pectin as too much will leave you with a set that is solid and unpalatable. Add a little at a time and keep checking the set, you can always add more pectin to achieve the set you desire, but you can't retract it if you add too much. Once the correct set is achieved pot up and seal.

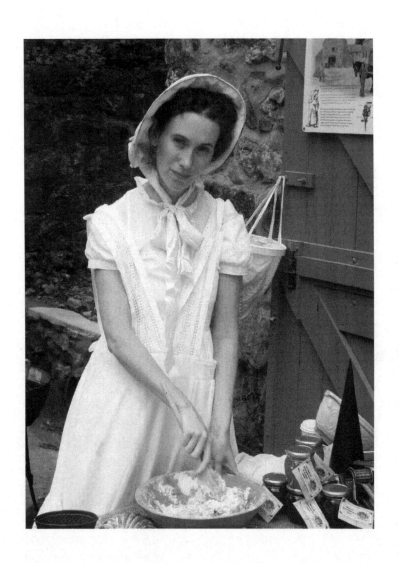

Chapter Three
The Curious Art of Chutney

Whilst overly sweet, over-processed, cloying commercially produced chutneys could be enough to put some people off for life. Making your own chutney is right up there with jam and bread making as the most satisfying and indulgent way to spend an afternoon. Once you have mastered chutney making it's quite possible that you will be spending every spare moment in the kitchen conjuring up new recipes and experimenting with new chutney sensations.

Whilst chutney making might seem like an insanely complicated dark-art at first glance they are easy and gratifying to make and they can make the dullest of sandwiches taste indulgent.

There is nothing better than opening a pantry door to find an array of taste-bud tickling chutneys at your disposal. No store cupboard can be thought of as complete without a selection of good chutneys for whether they are used to enrich casseroles, bejewel a simple supper or for adding depth to a curry they are definitely the cooks friend.

As chutneys mature with age they improve and there is a lot to be said for the traditional skill of chutney making. Traditionally chutneys are made at the height of summer and in the early autumn, because this is when the British garden produces bumper crops of fruit and vegetables, however, there is almost always something is season that will make a good base for a chutney and a good stock of chutneys will amply repay the work involved, which is not difficult if certain rules are followed.

There is no great mystery to unveil or great skills to master when it comes to chutney making. Chutneys are made with fruit and vegetables preserved with sugar and vinegar and enhanced with a variety of spices. Almost any fresh fruit whether ripe or unripe can be used and an exhaustive list of vegetable possibilities exists. The only rule on what to use is that whatever fruit or vegetables used in the chutney must be in good condition. Always avoid fruit and vegetables that are bruised or poor quality, it's a simple enough rule to remember: bad raw ingredients will lead to poor chutney.

Most chutneys are made from fruits with the addition of onion, but some vegetables such as runner beans and marrows make good chutneys too. It is also traditional for dried fruits to be added to chutneys as they bring rich flavours, depth and interest to the preserve. Apricots, raisins, sultanas, figs, apricots, mango, prunes and cherries all make excellent additions, but there is always room for experimentation.

As with all preserving methods; mouldy and rotting fruit or vegetables should be discarded. However, chutney is a traditional and excellent way of using up imperfect specimens of home-harvested fruit and windfalls once any bruises or damage are removed.

When choosing sugar for chutney it is important to think about the desired taste. Dark sugars such as Demerara and soft brown sugar will add colour as well as sweetness, whereas, paler, unrefined sugars will add flavours that will compliment fruits such as plums, apricots and eating apples. Similar choices are to made when choosing a vinegar, if a chutney is to be allowed time to mature before eating then malt vinegar is a good choice, it is relatively inexpensive and will do the trick, but chutneys made with this will need a long maturing time before they will become mellow enough to enjoy. These chutneys are seldom at their best until about six months after making, although most of them are palatable after two months.

For chutneys that are to be enjoyed immediately choosing a cider or wine vinegar will give the most agreeable results as they produce chutneys that need little if any time to mature. A well-made chutney can be kept for two years or longer and with maturity they generally improve, if only this were true of everything in life.

Both dried and fresh spices can be used in recipes, but the choice of spices used is particularly important in achieving the flavour combination you desire. The one rule to always follow is, that whether spices be whole or ground they should be as fresh as possible, yes that jar of allspice that has been lurking in the back of your cupboard has lost its potency and will not do your chutney justice.

Ground spices are generally preferred for chutneys because it is easier to adjust the flavouring as the mixture cooks. However, some cooks prefer to use whole spices, which should be crushed slightly and tied in a muslin bag, removing them at a late stage of the cooking.

If using fresh spices such as ginger and chillies bruise them first and then tie loosely in a muslin bag, which is tied to the pan handle and removed from the cooked chutney before potting.

Equipment

Making chutney doesn't require any specialist equipment and many of the things needed will be found in any cooks kitchen. A large capacity, heavy based pan that is made of a material that does not react with the vinegar is an absolute must. A stainless steel Maslin pan is ideal.

Reasonably accurate scales are needed for measuring out the chutney ingredients. Small muslin squares for putting your spices in are handy and a long handled wooden spoon completes the equipment list.

When choosing jars to pot your chutney up in, size and shape are not really important, but it is very important to ensure that a good seal is achieved and that the lids do not react with vinegar contact. Choose lids with a non-reactive coating and remember to label all your bottles with a name and date, otherwise you will spend a great deal of time pondering over the contents of similar looking jars of chutney.

Sterilising Jars

If the jars have been sterilised correctly and good hygiene practice employed the finished chutney will keep in a cool dark space for more than a year or two.

Technique

Chutney making is a labour of love that should be enjoyed and cannot be rushed. Indeed good chutney requires time and patience for chopping the fruit and vegetables by hand is time consuming, but the results that this process brings are infinitely superior to those achieved using a food processor, both in terms of appearance and texture.

Getting the Balance Right

You need to achieve the right balance of fruit, sugar and vinegar to achieve that quintessential sharp-sweet flavour and to preserve the chutney, so follow recipes carefully and weigh and measure everything. Once you've got to grips with the basic recipe formula, you can start to 'play' with the flavours and create your own special combinations. Every cook should have signature chutney to his or her name or at least a well-guarded recipe.

Autumn Chutney

The smell of this chutney makes me think of comfortable armchairs and nights in by a log fire. It's made at a time when we begin to prepare for winter and start to think of all things warming.

Ingredients:

450g plums
45g apples
45g tomatoes
45g onions
450g sultanas
600ml vinegar
¼ tsp. mixed spice
¼ tsp. ground ginger
450g Demerara sugar

Method:

Wash, peel, de-stone and chop the fruit and vegetables and place them all together in a large preserving pan with the spices and vinegar. Simmer over a medium heat for 30 minutes or until all the fruit and vegetables are tender.

Add the sugar and stir until dissolved. Simmer gently, stirring regularly, until the mixture becomes thick.

Cool slightly before ladling into warm jars and sealing.

Hot and Spicy Gooseberry Chutney

This chutney keeps well and is a great way to use up the last of the gooseberry harvest. Gooseberries on the under-ripe side work best in this recipe.

Ingredients:

1.35kg green gooseberries
450g onions
225g sultanas
25g fine rock salt
¼ tsp. turmeric
½ tsp. cayenne pepper
½ tsp. ground ginger
¼ tsp. cinnamon
25g chopped chillies
350g soft brown sugar
500ml white wine vinegar
6g yellow mustard seed

Method:

Wash, top and tail the gooseberries and place them in a large preserving pan.

Peel and finely chop the onions and add to the pan with all the other ingredients except the mustard seeds.

Bruise the mustard seed in a mortar and pestle and tie in a muslin bag. Add this spice bundle to the pan and stir well.

Heat very gently, stirring frequently, until sugar is dissolved.

Then bring to the boil and simmer gently, stirring regularly, for 1½ - 2 hours or until chutney is thick.

Remove the muslin spice bag and discard and pour the mixture into warm sterilised jars and seal.

Pumpkin Chutney

A tangy autumnal chutney that provides a warm glow on a cold and blustery day. Ideal with a strong cheddar cheese and delicious slathered over hot and bubbling cheese on toast.

Ingredients:

1.25kg pumpkin, prepared weight
500g ripe tomatoes
250g onions
125g sultanas
750g soft brown sugar
2½ tsp. ground ginger
2tsp ground black pepper
2 tsp. ground allspice
2 garlic cloves, crushed
2½ tbsp. salt
600ml cider vinegar

Method:

Peel and slice the tomatoes and onions and cut the pumpkin flesh into small pieces. Put all the vegetables in a preserving pan with the sultanas, sugar, spices, garlic, salt and vinegar. Stir over a gentle heat until all the sugar has dissolved. Bring to the boil and simmer gently until soft and the chutney is thick and jammy in consistency. Put into jars whilst still hot.

Rhubarb Chutney

A deep reddish amber coloured chutney that is perfect tucked inside a sandwich or as the finishing touch to curries, but by far it is the perfect companion to naughty nigh time snacks.

Ingredients:

2kg rhubarb
500g onions (diced)
500g soft brown sugar
600ml white wine vinegar
12.5 g salt
12.5g ground ginger
12.5 g medium curry powder

Method:

Prepare and chop the rhubarb and place in a preserving pan with the onions with half of the vinegar, salt, ginger and curry powder. Cook gently for approximately 1 hour and then add the remaining vinegar and the sugar, stir until the sugar is dissolved, simmer for a further 45 minutes to an hour. Ladle into prepared jars whilst still hot.

Rainy Day Chutney

Ideal for Making with Children

This is a no-cook recipe and is fantastic for making with little ones or as a quick way of perking up a cheeseboard. It is for eating not keeping, but nevertheless a great recipe for impromptu preserving.

Ingredients

2 large crisp apples, peeled, cored and diced
1 firm conference pear
1 red onion, finely chopped
125g sultanas
80ml red wine vinegar
40g dark brown soft sugar
½ tsp. ground ginger
¼ tsp. mixed spice

Method:

Mix all the ingredients together in a bowl. Give them a good stir and season generously with salt and pepper.

Pour into a sterilized jar and refrigerate. Leave for 2 - 3 days, shaking once a day, before eating. Keep for up to a week more.

Pear and Pumpkin Chutney

The pears in the recipe can be hard, ripe or a mixture of both. This is a great recipe for using up windfalls. Any firm fleshed squash can be used including pumpkin, butternut squash and acorn.

Ingredients:

1 kg pears, peeled, cored and roughly diced.
500g of pumpkin or squash, peeled, seeded and diced

500g onions diced
500g raisins
2 cloves garlic, peeled and crushed
5cm fresh ginger, peeled and finely chopped
500g brown sugar
750 ml cider vinegar.
1 tsp. salt
1tsp allspice berries
1 stick cinnamon.

Method:

Place the chopped pears, squash, onions and raisins into a preserving or large heavy based pan. In a mortar and pestle combine the garlic and ginger with a splash of vinegar to make a paste. Add to the paste to the pan, followed by the salt, vinegar and sugar. Tie the allspice berries and cinnamon stick in a piece of muslin and tie to the pan handle.

Put the pan on a medium heat and stir frequently until the sugar has dissolved. Cook the mixture slowly, stirring frequently as it thickens so that it doesn't stick to the base and burn. When it is well cooked, remove the spice bag and pot the chutney in sterilised jars. Once the chutney is made all that remains is to find new and interesting ways to eat it, or simply enjoy it with a good hunk of cheddar cheese and some homemade bread.

Green Tomato Chutney

A tangy and spicy chutney that makes a wonderful accompaniment to curries and salads alike.

Ingredients:

500g green tomatoes
500g onions
500g apples
500g brown sugar
568 ml distilled white vinegar
½ tsp. mixed spice
1 tsp. dry mustard
½ tsp. Strong curry powder
2 tsp. salt

Method:

Finely chop the tomatoes, apples and onions. Put them in an earthenware bowl and sprinkle with the salt. Cover and leave somewhere cool overnight.

Strain off the resulting liquor and discard. Rinse the vegetables in a colander. Put the remains of the onion, tomato, apple mix into a pan and add the vinegar, spice, mustard, ginger and pepper. Bring to the boil and simmer for about 1½ hours, stirring occasionally to stop the mixture from sticking to the base of the saucepan.

Turn off the heat and leave it in the pan to cool. Once it is at room temperature then ladle it into clean jars, seal and put to one side for use. This can be eaten immediately after cooking, but you will find that the flavour improves if left for four weeks to mature.

When Things Go Wrong

Shrinkage in the jar

If you find that your chutney shrinks in the jar after storage this is because a good airtight seal has not been achieved, allowing the moisture to evaporate. The chutney will be fine to eat. In future always make sure a good seal has been achieved by tightening lids after twenty four hours.

Liquid has collected on top of the chutney

If liquid collects on top of the chutney whilst it is in store it might be because it hasn't been cooked out enough. It is possible to rectify this, firstly you need to sterilise fresh jars ready for re- potting afterwards. Empty the chutney back in to the jam pan and bring it to the boil. Allow the chutney to boil until the excess liquid has evaporated. Re-pot and seal your jars and store.

Chutney is Runny

If the chutney is very runny with a lot of liquid in comparison to vegetables then this is again down to it not having been cooked long enough for the excess liquid to have evaporated. Follow the steps detailed above for rectifying, 'liquid has collected on top of the chutney'.

Chapter Four
In a Pickle

Lip smarting, salty, crisp and spicy are just some of the words that go towards describing a good jar of pickled vegetables. There is nothing quite like taking a bite into a perfectly crisp, pickled onion, these dark golden gems, shining brightly from their vinegar filled jars are the treasure of the British larder. Whilst there are hundreds of commercial brands of pickle on the market nothing beats a good home-made pickle and the crunch of a perfectly prepared home-preserved pickled gherkin.

There is a time when pickling was of great importance to every household. A time when winters were long and grim affairs in which fresh produce was a rarity, that's if it were available at all. A winter diet mainly consisted of pickled food in one form or another.

Pickled fish, vegetables and fruits as well as salted and smoked meats were things that would be made with pride and skill in the household kitchen.

The industrious and ingenious housewife would make her preserves, brew beer, cider, mead, wine and put down her pickles. Pickles and preserves were laid down with care to take care of future needs. This was a time when a household was a self-contained, self-sufficient unit.

'if only it grew on trees...

Brining... soaking in brine is best for produce with a low water content.

Hot pickling

Cold pickling

I start life as a cucumber and become a delicious pickle.

Pickle.

In a **PICKLE!!**

PICKLE POWER!

Perfect Pickled Gherkins

500g small pickling cucumbers
125g sea salt
4 shallots
4 garlic cloves
1/2 tsp. coriander seeds
1/2 tsp. pink peppercorns
1/2 tsp. dill seeds
a vine leaf for extra crunch

NOTE Rub the cucumbers down with a cloth to remove their down before salting.

METHOD

Trim the cucumbers & clean them. In a ceramic bowl place a layer of cucumbers and cover with salt. Keep repeating! Leave for 24 hrs. — THIS WILL EXTRACT THE LIQUID GIVING LOVELY CRISP PICKLES!

Wash the cucumbers thoroughly in cold water to remove excess salt. Pack cucumbers in sterilised jars, leaving 1cm head-room. Pour in enough vinegar to cover the cucumbers completely.

Larders and stillrooms were full of tasty preserved food and there was always a basis of a meal tucked away in these wondrous rooms.

With the rise of industry, came cheap and efficient transport in the form of railways and this suddenly made fresh fish available to everyone and the death of fish pickling.

The discovery and development of the canning technique gave a heavy blow to the art of pickling and refrigeration was the green light to mass production and a near fatal blow to pickling. Whilst advancements in food technology have served to enhance our diet, but all good things can be overdone and mass production has led to monotony. Variety is said to be the spice of life and a well-stocked pantry and the ability to explore variations in food and discover lost arts is only going to lead to a more inspired diet.

Pickling is an art worth mastering and once you have made your own piccalilli sauce adding just the right amount of turmeric to make a rich yellow sauce evolve as vivid as a sunset and as rich as butter ; once you have breathed in the sweet, sour, rich, tantalizing notes of a home-made pickle there is no turning back, shop bought will never do again.

Pickled Eggs

Delicious, nutty brown eggs delicately spiced are best served with fresh bread and a pint of Britain's finest real ale.

Sadly when most people think of pickled eggs, I am sure they picture those anaemic examples lurking in huge jars full of vinegar at the back of the fish and chip shop next to the pickled onions. They can be piquant, subtly spiced and certainly mellow enough to eat on their own or in salads and nothing like the chip shop version.

Ingredients

Hen's or quail's eggs
1 litre (2 pints) of white wine or cider vinegar
3 or 4 dried red chillies
15 g (½ oz.) fresh ginger, peeled and thinly sliced
15 g (½ oz.) brown mustard seeds
15 g (½ oz.) peppercorns, black or white
10 g (⅓ oz.) coriander seeds

Method:

First, select enough eggs that you think will fill snugly inside your jars, but remember not to pack too tightly as there has to be room for the vinegar. Put them in a pan with cold water and bring them to a boil. Simmer the eggs until hard-boiled; this means just 2 minutes for quail's eggs up to 12 minutes for large hen's eggs. Once cooked immediately rinse under cold, running water. Once cold, carefully peel off the shells and place into the prepared jars.

Make the pickling liquor by pouring the vinegar into a saucepan. Add the spices and bring to a simmer for five minutes. Strain, then cover and let cool.

Cover the eggs with the pickling liquor, making sure that the eggs are completely covered. Place a few of the spices in each of the jars and seal tightly.

Leave the eggs for about 2 weeks in a cool, dark place and then enjoy!

Pickled Onions:

The world of food would be a sad place without pickled onions. Good pickled onions are crisp, crunchy and full of flavour; they make bread and cheese a meal. More importantly they are an essential part of that great traditional British dish: The Ploughman's Lunch. Most commercially produced pickled onions are a pale imitation of this delicious pickle lacking crunch and bite.

When making pickled onions a carefully blended selection of pickling spices is essential, it's worth blending your own or buying the best you can get.

Ingredients:

500g small shallots
50g salt
500ml malt vinegar
200g brown sugar
5 bay leaves
2 tsp. pickling spices

Method:

Place the onions in a large heatproof bowl and pour over boiling water to cover. Leave to cool. Once cool, trim roots and tops and peel. Sprinkle the salt over the peeled onions, stir and leave overnight.

The next day rinse the onions with cold water, removing as much salt as possible and dry with a clean cotton tea towel. Place the spices vinegar and sugar into a large pan and gently heat just to dissolve the sugar into the vinegar, but do not boil. Pack the onions into clean, sterilised jars. Pour over the hot vinegar mixture to fill the jars, and check there are no air pockets. Seal the jars and leave to cool. The onions will be ready to eat after about one month or better if kept for longer. Once opened store in the fridge.

Pub Style Pickled Onions

This recipe makes the type of strong and crunchy pickled onions that are the staple ingredient of traditional Christmas gatherings and real British country inns.

Ingredients:

500g rock salt.
1kg pickling onions.
2 litres malt vinegar.
Pickling spices
Bay leaves

Method:

Mix one litre of boiling water with the salt and let it cool, stirring until the salt has partially dissolved. Peel the shallots or onions, place in a large bowl and cover with the salt water. Cover the bowl with a plate and weight down to make sure all the onions are fully submerged. Leave for 24 hours. Put vinegar, sugar and pickling spices into a saucepan and bring to the boil – you can get ready mixed pickling spices at most health food shops and supermarkets, but you may choose to make your own mixture of finely chopped red chilli, peppercorns, coriander seeds, mustard seeds and dried herbs. Sniff your pickling mixture carefully as this really can make your eyes water and result in a coughing fit. I like to leave the spices in the mixture because they look pretty and they continue to add flavour, but you can sieve it if you prefer.

Rinse the onions thoroughly and dry. Pack onions into hot, sterilised jars, leaving 1 inch space to top of lid. Drop a bay leaf into each jar for added flavour and prettiness.

Cap jars tightly and store in a cool place – Brilliant for a traditional Christmas or a sunny afternoon with a pint of real ale or cider.

Pickled Apricots

This pickle looks glorious and the natural sweetness of the apricots is given a fabulous tang when preserved in this way. An absolute must with festive buffets and British cheeseboards.

Ingredients:

375ml white wine vinegar
275g sugar
500g fresh apricots
1 small cinnamon stick

Method:

Pour the vinegar into a preserving pan, add the sugar and heat gently, stirring until the sugar has dissolved. Once all the sugar has dissolved bring to the boil.

Peel the apricots. The easiest way to loosen the apricots skins is to bring a large pot of water to the boil.

When it's reached a rolling boil drop in your fruit. Leave them for about a minute and then transfer them to a cold water bath (a deep bowl or bucket filled with very cold water). Now, a quick little rub should have those skins falling away and you're fruit will be ready to pickle.

Pack the apricots into a large, sterilised jar as tightly as possible, add the cinnamon stick to the jar and carefully pour in the hot vinegar syrup. Cover immediately.

Leave to mature for at least a month.

Elderberry Pickle

This is superb stuff and quite unlike any other pickle, its deep rich purple makes you think of winter months and indeed it's an excellent accompaniment to winter warmers such as roast venison, pheasant and full bodied cheeses.

Ingredients:

500g elderberries
2 tbsp. sugar
1 small onion
½ tsp. ground ginger
½ tsp. ground mixed spice
300 ml vinegar
Pinch of salt

Method:

Wash all the berries and remove the stalks. Give the berries a thorough mashing. Place all the ingredients in a pan and bring to the boil. Cook over a low heat, slowly, until the mixture thickens. Stir so that the mixture does not stick and burn. Once nice and thick, put into prepared jars whilst still hot.

Old Fashioned Fig Pickle

A rich and spicy pickle that is delicious served with pork and cold meats. Makes an excellent addition to The Ploughman's Lunch or added to lamb dinner, but in my opinion it is best served next to rich, sumptuous goats cheese and makes a great topping for cheese tarts of all varieties.

Ingredients:

500g dried figs
Pickling mixture:
300ml vinegar
500g Demerara sugar
1 tbsp. ground cloves
1 tbsp. ground cinnamon
1 tsp. ground mace
1 tsp. allspice

Method:

Wash the figs in cold water and then leave them to soak overnight in a basin of cold water. The next day drain them in a colander and set them aside.

To make the pickling mixture, boil the sugar and pickling vinegar, stirring until the sugar dissolves and the mixture becomes thick. Add the cloves, cinnamon, mace and allspice. Simmer for a minute or two, then add the figs and cook gently for an hour. Place into prepared jars whilst hot.

THE LARDER

There is no finer sight than a larder in autumn. Rows of malted gold onions, gleaming from their glass jars

What makes a good pickle? Crispy crunchy sweet sour tasty moreish

I ♥ You more than Pickles

use good vinegar! Check that it has acetic acid content of at least 5%

HAPPY PICKLE

IN A PICKLE!

Sweet water melon Rind pickle — rather a bizarre idea but very tasty

Damson Pickle

This will keep for years and keeps on improving with age. Fabulous added to game pies and casseroles or served with cheeses or cold meats.

Ingredients

4lbs (2kg) damsons
3lbs (1.5kg) Demerara sugar
½ pint (300ml) vinegar
1 cinnamon stick

Method:

Place the cinnamon and cloves in a muslin bag and place in a pan with the sugar and vinegar. Boil for 10 minutes and remove the spices. Add the fruit and boil for ten minutes. Be careful not to break up and mush the fruit whilst stirring. Place into a large jar and seal.

Pickled Nasturtium Seeds

Nutty and peppery these seeds are well worth preserving. Described by some as poor man's capers, these wonderful little seeds liven up any canapé or salad, not mention their potential in soups and sauces.

Ingredients:

70 g Nasturtium seeds (you want the fresh, green seeds for this.)
600ml white wine vinegar
2 bay leaves
2tsp. salt
6 peppercorns

Method:

Pick through the seeds to remove the flower petals, rinse seeds in cold water and spread on a tray and dry in a very slow oven. In a small non-reactive saucepan place the bay leaves, peppercorns and salt with the vinegar and bring boil. Remove from the heat and allow to cool before straining.

Place the clean, dry Nasturtium seeds into sterilised jars and pour the infused vinegar over the top. Seal the jar and keep for at least two months before using.

They are wonderful tossed on salads that have fresh Nasturtium flowers added for colour, or added to canapés

Ploughman's Pickle

This is an all-round pickle. It's incredibly versatile and if you only intend to make one pickle then this would be a good one to opt for. Serve with cheese, ploughman's lunches, in sandwiches, with cold cuts and meats; add it to stews, casseroles and curries. There are endless possibilities for this sweet and tangy pickle.

Ingredients:

255g carrots, peeled and cut into small chunks
1 medium swede, peeled and cut into small chunks
4 -5 garlic cloves, peeled and finely chopped
140g dates, finely chopped
1 small cauliflower, finely chopped
2 onions, peeled and finely chopped
2 medium apples, finely chopped, unpeeled
2 medium finely chopped courgettes, unpeeled
15 -20 small gherkins, finely chopped
285g dark brown sugar
1 tsp. salt
4 tbsp. lemon juice
426ml malt vinegar
2 tsp. mustard seeds
2 tsp. ground allspice
1 tsp. cayenne pepper

Method:

Combine all the ingredients in a large saucepan and bring them to the boil. Then reduce the heat to a simmer and cook until the swede is cooked, but still remains firm, about 2 hours. Stir well to combine all the vegetables. Ladle the pickle into sterilised jars and seal.

Allow the pickle to age for a few weeks before using, this improves the taste and it will become quite mellow.

Pickled Quinces

As soon as the clocks go back the quince starts to appear in good greengrocers. This beautiful deep yellow fruit is an absolute treasure that is frequently overlooked, perhaps because it has to be cooked before eating. Its soft and haunting perfume and hedonistic flesh marks the start of winter and of all things deep and comforting. The quince flavour is rich and aromatic with a heady perfume and subdued sweetness. A fruit of generous curves with a perfect complexion and a touch of the forbidden about it.

Quinces like all good cooks love a glass or two of something comfortingly alcoholic and I love to sprinkle halved quinces with brown sugar and a slosh of Masala and bake in the oven, but the quince can be made into a fabulous pickle with a delicate spice, sweetness and gentle acidity.

Soulful, sensual and spirited, there is nothing quite like a delicious pickled quince to serve up with cold meats and good strong British cheeses.

Ingredients:

750ml cider vinegar
400g golden granulated sugar
3 medium-sized quinces or 4 smaller ones
10 pink peppercorns
1 cinnamon stick
4 star anise
1 bay leaf

Method:

Pour the vinegar into a stainless-steel or other non-reactive pan. Add the golden sugar, cinnamon, star anise, peppercorns and bay leaf and bring to the boil. Turn the heat down to a steady, bubbling simmer.

Peel, halve and core the quinces, cutting them into six lengthways. Gently place the quince into the simmering vinegar and leave the fruit to cook for 15-25 minutes, until it is soft yet still holding together.

Gently Lift the soft fruits out with a slotted spoon and lower them into clean, sterilised storage jars. Pour over the hot liquor, then seal and leave to cool. They will keep for several weeks and rarely last for long.

Victorian Bullace Pickle

The tangy sweet-sour flavour and rich, ruddy colour of wild plums is captured in this wonderful whole fruit pickle.

Ingredients:

1.5kg bullace (wild plums)

600ml of white wine vinegar
Spice bundle: star anise, cinnamon and allspice tied in muslin
750g Demerara sugar

Method:

Pack the washed bullace into preserving jars and place in a moderate oven and cook until the skins begin to slit. Boil the vinegar with the spice bag and the sugar for ten minutes, then remove the spices, and pour over the bullace. Cover the jars when cold.

In a Pickle…when things don't turn out as expected

Soft pickles

If your pickles are soft when you come to eat them this may be down to using vinegar with low acidity or not enough salt. Make sure to measure salt carefully and choose vinegar which has 5-7% acid content. Another cause for soft pickles is storing them in a place which is too warm. Make sure to store pickles in a cool, dry and dark place.

Tough pickles

Whereas too little salt causes soft pickles, too much salt causes tough pickles so take care to measure the correct amount as indicated by your recipe. Tough pickles can also occur by processing them for too long so be sure to time correctly.

Dark coloured Pickles

Pickles can become dark if ground spices are used instead of whole spices. Darkening can also occur if table salt is used as it contains anti-caking agents which cause discolouration. It is always advisable to use good quality rock salt. Finally, the water used to make the brine may be hard; the ideal water for making the brine is soft or distilled water.

Mouldy Pickles

If your pickles are mouldy when you come to eat them you must discard them immediately as they are not edible. The next time you pickle be sure to take extra care over sterilisation of jars and lids or seals and make sure a good airtight seal has formed. Also make sure you wash each vegetable thoroughly before processing. Unlike preserves these vegetables are not cooked so washing them is important.

Discolouration of Pickles

If your pickles start to discolour in the jar make sure you are storing them correctly. Exposure to direct sunlight can cause discolouration, so always choose a dark, well ventilated, cool place for storage.

Chapter Five
Marvellous Marmalade

Marmalade to me is like a jar of winter sunshine, it comes in various shades of orange from dark and chunky to bright orange with thin shreds of peel suspended like strands of glistening tinsel. There is just something about a bright, sparkling jar of marmalade that makes me smile and fills me with glee.

Marmalade has a long history and has many peaks and troughs in its popularity, but it's not toast yet. After a post-World War II decline in consumption, marmalade is now undergoing a comeback in Britain. Many home cooks continue to make their own, often using precious heirloom recipes that are treasured and passed down through generations.

Because Seville oranges are only available for a short season from late December through to February, marmalade-making is a seasonal ritual. The enduring tradition that revolves around just three simple ingredients, water, sugar and Seville oranges which yields a symbol of iconic Britishness. Marmalade is to Britain is a necessity, an identifier and a constant reminder of our history, Marmalade is part of the British psyche.

There is evidence that Britain had a sort of quince marmalade called chardequince from around the time of the Battle of Agincourt. This was really a quince paste and the term marmalade was a generic name that referred to fruit pastes. These thick quince pastes were flavoured with red wine, honey, cinnamon and ginger and were taken at the end of a feast, along with fruit, nuts, and other sweetmeats whose purpose was to ease the stomach and aid digestion.

Today in Europe, the term "marmalade" and its variations is still used as a generic term, while in Britain we've redefined it as referring solely to a citrus preserve. The Oxford dictionary defines marmalade as follows: 'a preserve made from citrus fruit, especially bitter oranges.' Although plenty of early recipes still exist for marmalade that challenge the citrus fruits claim of ownership.

There are many foods that littered our ancestors tables that have fell from our modern culinary repertoire, so why do we still love marmalade so dearly? Is it because it just has so much history and has continued to evolve and change. Indeed Mary Queen of Scots used a quince marmalade to cure sea-sickness , "Marmelade pour Marie malade" , whilst Mary Tudor used a marmalade made of quinces, orange peel, sugar, almonds, rosewater, musk, ambergris, cinnamon, cloves, ginger and mace to aid her fertility, and give her hope of bearing a son. Sadly it didn't work and she died childless, but marmalade had long been considered an aphrodisiac.

An explanation of the unusual name for this orange preserve is that the quince pastes imported into Britain were known in their varying forms as marmalades (from the Portuguese 'marmelo' – quince), but a more unlikely explanation of the name exists, suggesting that Mary Queen of Scots was served a rudimentary version to help overcome a crippling vitamin C deficiency. In this telling, the name is a shortened version of 'Mary, my Lady'. Whatever, the name and whenever it gained its name the fact remains that marmalade is incredibly satisfying to make. Doing something carefully, and well, enriches the soul and in the winter, the darkest time of the year, longing for winter sun can be quelled as the heady smell of cooking oranges fills the house like the scent of a giant pomander.

Versions of quince marmalade became a staple of "banquetting stuffe," the elegant display of sweetmeats and confectionery served at the end of 16th- and 17th-century English feasts.

These decorative quince pastes were a feast for the eyes and stomach.

Although orange marmalade has been made in England since the late Tudor period, it is by the Victorian era our current notion of marmalade in which the bitter Seville oranges are tempered by the sweetness of the sugar to produce a fresh yet intensely rich orange fragrance emerges.

Undoubtedly marmalade is now part of the eccentric British culture, it is woven into our heritage and is here to stay. Jars of it travelled the world with colonial administrators throughout the days of the British Empire. Queen Victoria's grand-daughters had it sent to them when they became the Empress of Russia and the Queen of Greece. When English explorer Robert Scott ventured to the Antarctic in 1911-12, he carried among his provisions, marmalade. So did Sir Edmund Hillary when he scaled Mount Everest in 1953. Even the fictional James Bond, better known for a shaken martini has his daily breakfast regime of a boiled egg, toast with butter and marmalade.

Marmalade is in our hearts, in our literature and popular culture. We have been raised on stories about Paddington Bear who likes nothing better than a marmalade sandwich and even our pop culture cannot escape from the stuff, think back to the lyrics of The Beatles', "Lucy in the Sky with Diamonds", with its, "marmalade skies". It seems that we Brits just can't get marmalade out of our thoughts.

Like many historical foods there are always myths and stories about how they came to be. One such story is that marmalade is a Scottish invention that can be attributed to Janet Keiller in 1797, a Dundee grocer's wife. The story goes that marmalade was born in the port of

Dundee in the late 18th century when a local victualler, James Keiller discovered a cargo of oranges being sold cheaply. Thinking he could sell it for profit in his shop, he bought the whole cargo, only to discover the oranges were bitter and therefore unsalable in their raw state. In despair his wife, Janet took them home with the idea of making a jam. The resulting "jam" was hugely successful and was named Marmalade after Marmelos, the Portuguese word for a quince paste similar in texture to the orange spread. Another wonderful fictional twist on this story is the fruit being carried up from the beach by Janet's son, who was sent back to get more oranges with his mother urging 'Mair, ma lad!' this is where the product's name originated in accordance with this fable.

Dr William Mathew of the University of East Anglia who has extensively researched the Keiller Marmalade Company points out that James Keiller of the marmalade-producing company was still a bachelor at the close of the 18th century and that Janet was his mother, not his wife. He also points out that single fruit shipments were rare and so if there was a cargo of Seville oranges is was more likely to have been a few boxes.

Whilst the "invention" of orange marmalade is erroneously attributed Janet Keiller , the Keillier Marmalade Company was among the first of a series of late 18th- and early 19th-century grocers who established commercial marmalade factories to meet the demand for store-bought marmalade that had grown and they did introduce 'chip' marmalade, the form of the preserve we recognise today. Marmalade, prior to the Keillers' involvement, had been around in various forms for centuries it is not so much any ones invention as a product of organic evolution.

By the late 19th century, numerous British firms produced marmalades for every preference, ranging from Robertson's fine-cut Golden and Silver Shred to Frank Cooper's coarse-cut "Oxford" marmalade, to Chivers'

Olde English, which was marketed as "The Aristocrat of Marmalades." Wilkin of Tiptree, an English fruit conserving company founded in 1885, was producing some 27 different marmalades by the turn of the 20th century, according to the preeminent marmalade scholar, C. Anne Wilson, who authored "The Book of Marmalade'.

Not all marmalade makers have continued to enjoy success, The London based company Descastro & Peach gave up making marmalade after their product was tested in the 1850s, and was found to contain children's toe-nails & high levels of copper from over-boiling in copper vessels.

No matter what the origins, real marmalade brings brightness to the dullest of days. I don't think any commercial marmalade can substitute the joy of making it yourself. As soon as you begin to make marmalade it is therapy for the senses, the smell of sticky, bittersweet orange marmalade will linger in every corner of the kitchen. To breathe is to inhale the rich pleasures of unadulterated gluttony. It is all you can do to surrender to the pleasure that is marmalade making. In an instance the scent of zesty top notes can transport you to summers filled with endless good weather and endless possibilities. Marmalade making is magical and the tradition of marmalade is endless.

Freshly potted jars of home-made marmalade are as rich as butter and the colour of the finest Baltic amber. Not only is the process addictive and all-consuming, but the end result is pots of sunshine that will fill breakfast times with joy and cakes with a touch of brilliance.

Home-made marmalade versus shop bought isn't to do with snobbery and following the foodie trend it's to do with the experience, because as you begin the process of juicing Seville oranges you find that you cherish each drop of bitter sweet juice. Cutting the skin into thin strands allows you time to wallow in the smell of balmy weather and happiness, breathing in every bittersweet spray of zest. Relax and breathe deeply as you enjoy the prickle of the fruit oil on your skin and the awakening of your senses as the scent of orange nectar fills the air. There is no better treat for the olfactory system than marmalade in the making.

As your tongue tingles at the taste of oranges so clean, crisp and sharp, agitating your taste buds and making you salivate, you know you have discovered something magical. Your mind races with excitement as your senses dance to the ancient art of marmalade making; surely so much pleasure in a kitchen should be forbidden.

As your house fills with a sweet lingering smell; that is heart-warmingly generous, familiar and as comforting as a log fire on a cold night. The sound of bubbling oranges in copper pans cannot adequately describe this simple pleasure. The glimmer of marmalade in creation, soft and syrupy putting any attempt at molecular gastronomy to shame. Watching the mixture of peel; juice, pith, water and sugar transforming into rich, golden jars of shining; bittersweet happiness.

With the excitement and nervous expectation of an adolescent girl on a first date you test for the setting point. Using your index finger to push the edges of the marmalade on a cold plate, awaiting the desired wrinkle and crinkle denoting a perfect set. A feeling of achievement quite unlike any other washes over you as you gaze at the ripple of wrinkled marmalade on a saucer, indeed you can now pronounce yourself a Marmalade Goddess.

Carefully decanting your liquid gold into prepared jars, as the rain taps on your kitchen window and the winter sky turns grey; you can think of warm sunshine, the scent of almond and orange blossom mixing gently with that of evening jasmine and can think of no greater pleasure than your annual escape to Marmalade Club, an exclusive club that takes place every year in the solitude of your own kitchen. Signalled by the arrival of those coarse skinned Seville oranges just after Christmas.

This is not preserve making that we are talking about this is about preserving a quintessential part of British history, it's about keeping an ancient art in practice and it about a simple recipe that means that the right amounts of fruit, sugar and water produces a clear jelly with a slightly loose "set," and a clear, bright flavour. Britain has every reason to be obsessed with the stuff.

Handy Tips on Marmalade Making:

- Make sure you have a large enough pan to hold all the liquid and peel with plenty of extra space.
- When peeling the skins, keep the pieces as large as possible to make chopping easier.
- Don't over-boil the marmalade once set or the marmalade will be too solid.
- If you are not confident peeling the skin from the whole fruit with a knife, cut the fruit into quarters, squeeze out the juice (reserve the juice for the pan and add any pips that come out into the muslin bag). Scrape the inner flesh, pips, and white pith away from the skin with a knife or teaspoon and put in the muslin bag. Chop the peel for the pan as above.
- Never use caster sugar when making marmalade, it will just sink to the bottom of the pan, instead use granulated sugar.
- Always warm your sugar on a baking sheet in the oven before adding it to your marmalade pan.
- Make sure that your rind is soft before adding the sugar, for once the sugar is added the rind will not soften any further.

Thick Quince Marmalade

A deep red amber colour this marmalade has a thick texture and unique taste.

Ingredients:

500g quinces
350g sugar

Cold water

Method:

Wash the quinces and slice as thinly as possible. Place the fruit in a preserving pan and cover with enough cold water to just cover the fruit. Simmer gently for 40 minutes and then pass the pulp through a sieve to separate the fruit from the pips.

Return the pulp to a clean pan and add the sugar. Stir over a medium heat, until the sugar has dissolved. Simmer gently for 15 minutes or until the setting point is reached. This mixture catches and burns easily so make sure you stir it regularly.

Pot in warm jars and seal whilst hot.

Tudor Marmalade

Tudor housewives taught themselves to make marmelada/marmalade at home, and the name became applied to the method of preserving fruit, and not just to one type of fruit. 16th century recipe books record cooking instructions for apple, pear and strawberry marmalades. Quinces were popular because they are naturally high in pectin, which means the fruit helps the marmalade to set readily. This recipe produces a thick, rich and robust and deep wine coloured preserve. This marmalade is much darker and heavier in consistency than Portuguese marmelada and Spanish membrillo.

You will need a wooden box for this recipe, something like an old Turkish Delight box is ideal. Line it with greaseproof paper so that the marmalade doesn't stick.

Ingredients:

2 quinces,
sugar,
water

Method:

Wash the quinces and then gently stew them whole, using just enough water to cover them. . They are ready when the skin tears readily when prodded with a spoon handle, this usually takes around an hour to achieve. Remove the fruit from the water, but don't discard. Let the fruit cool a little, and when you the fruit is cool enough to handle, peel, core and slice them. Now weigh them and weigh out an equal amount of sugar. Return the sliced fruit to the pan of water used to stew them, and add the sugar. Put the pan over a very low heat, cover, and leave for six to seven hours for the water to reduce and the quinces to take on a rich, deep and beautiful red colour. Once ready, ladle into your prepared wooden box and cover.

Oxford Marmalade

This marmalade is slightly darker in colour because of the treacle and brown sugar but great to make when Seville oranges are in season. Stock up your cupboards with this delicious, traditional marmalade

Ingredients:

6 small Seville oranges, well washed
3 lemons, well washed
2.5 litres water

450g granulated sugar
320g brown sugar
60g black treacle

Method:

Cut the oranges and lemons in half, squeeze the juice and strain it into a stainless-steel or enamel preserving pan. Using your fingers, remove all the flesh and pips from the squeezed fruit and tie the pips securely in a muslin square with the halves of lemon peel. Cut the orange peel pieces in half, then crossways into strips about 5 mm thick. Add the strips and the muslin bag to the pan pour in the water and bring to the boil. Reduce the heat and simmer for 2 hours, or until the peel is very soft and the liquid has been reduced by half. Remove the muslin bag from the pan, put it in a bowl and leave until cool enough to handle. Squeeze the bag to remove as much juice as possible, and then pour the juice back into the pan. Discard the bag. Add the sugars and treacle to the pan and stir over medium heat until the sugar has dissolved. Bring to a full rolling boil and boil for 15–20 minutes. Remove from the heat and test if setting point has been reached. When the marmalade has set, skim any scum from the surface. Leave the marmalade to stand for 20 minutes to allow the peel to settle. Stir to disperse the peel evenly, then pour into clean, warm, dry jars and cover the jars with waxed paper discs and cellophane covers. When cold, label and store in a cool, dark, airy cupboard.

Ginger Marmalade

A refreshing change from orange marmalade. It's delicious on wheaten bread or treacle scones or you can stir a few tablespoons into a fruit crumble for added zing. It's also delicious with savoury dishes like baked ham or sticky ribs.

Ingredients:

315g very fresh ginger
950ml water
1kg caster sugar
85g liquid pectin
Sterilised jars and lids

Method:

Peel the ginger root and divide it in half; chop half into cubes and grate the other half. Place the ginger into a large saucepan with water over medium heat, bring to a boil, and reduce heat to a simmer. Cover the pot, and simmer the ginger until tender, about 1 hour and 15 minutes. Add more water if needed to keep mixture from drying out. Pour the cooked ginger through a sieve and retain 120ml of the ginger-flavoured water. Place the cooked ginger in a bowl with the retained liquid, and cool at least 4 hours or overnight in fridge. 3. When ginger is thoroughly cooled, place into a large, heavy-bottomed pot, and stir in the sugar; bring to the boil over medium-high heat, and boil hard for 1 minute, stirring constantly. Stir in the liquid pectin, reduce the heat to very low and cook for 10 more minutes, stirring and skimming foam from top of marmalade. 4. Spoon into clean, sterilised jam jars and tightly seal with appropriate lids. Store in fridge or a cool, dark cupboard

Pumpkin Marmalade

This pumpkin marmalade with orange makes a great gift, if you can bring yourself to give it away. It is so very delicious.

Ingredients:

3 oranges
1.8kg pumpkin
500ml water
1.8kg sugar

Method:

Slice oranges finely. Peel pumpkin, remove the seeds and cut into small cubes. Place oranges in a saucepan and cover with water. Add pumpkin to another saucepan and cover with sugar. Let stand for 24 hours. Bring oranges to the boil, and then add to pumpkin and sugar. Boil slowly until tender. Ladle into sterilised jars.

Mixed Citrus Marmalade

This is a zingy marmalade that can be made at any time of year - a sweet gel with tangy strands of lemon and lime. Be warned it's very moreish A few jars kept at home on a larder shelf would give you a taste of summery freshness during those short dark winter days.

Ingredients:

900g oranges or a mixture of oranges and grapefruit
2 lemons

1.75kg granulated sugar

Method:

Wash the fruit, then halve and squeeze the juice into a preserving pan or large, heavy-based stainless steel saucepan. Tie the pips and membranes in a muslin bag. Cut the peel into thin shreds (or coarse ones, if preferred) and then add to the saucepan with the bag of pips and 2.25 litres of water. Bring to the boil, then simmer gently, uncovered for about 2 hours or until the contents of the pan are reduced by about half and the peel is soft and tender. Remove the muslin bag, leave to cool, and then squeeze any liquid back into the pan. Add the sugar to the saucepan and stir over a very low heat, until completely dissolved. Bring to the boil and boil rapidly for about 15 minutes or until setting point is reached (105°C on a sugar thermometer). Remove the saucepan from the heat and skim off any scum from the surface with a wooden spoon. Leave to cool, for about 5 minutes, or until a thin skin starts to form on top of the marmalade. Stir gently, to distribute the peel evenly. Ladle into warm, sterilised jars, then cover and seal. When cold, label, then store in a cool dark place. Use within 1 year of making. Once opened, store in the fridge and use within 1 month.

Blood Orange and Rosemary Marmalade

A bold and fresh marmalade that can be used for sweet and savoury purposes alike.

Ingredients:

2.5 lbs. blood oranges

2 large lemons
6 cups cold water
8 cups sugar
6 good sized sprigs rosemary wrapped in a single layer of muslin and tied to make a bag.

Method:

Thoroughly wash oranges and lemons. Slice in half vertically, place cut side down, and then slice into thin half-moons. Remove seeds as you come across them. Place slices in a large pot and cover with the water. Let soak at room temperature for 12 to 24 hours. (This releases the pectin and softens the rind) The next day, bring the pot to a boil and boil steadily for 30 minutes. Stir in the sugar and rosemary bundle and cook at a steady boil until the mixture has softly jellied, if the setting point has not been reached, boil for another five minutes and test again.

Remove rosemary bundle from marmalade. Ladle the hot marmalade into the prepared jars, filling about ¼ inch from the top.

Emergency Marmalade

If you should ever find the cupboard bare of marmalade and the Seville orange season all but a distant memory, then an emergency marmalade recipe is called for.

Ingredients:

2 sweet oranges
2 large grapefruits
10 lemons

10 pints of water
6lbs sugar

Method:

This is quick fix marmalade so start my juicing all the fruit and reserving the pips. Either put the fruit through a mincer or slice it up thinly. Soak the prepared fruit in the juice and water for 48 hrs. Tie up the pips in muslin and refrigerate until needed. After soaking, place the fruit, its liquid and the bag of pips into a pan and boil for two hours, after which the fruit should be soft. Remove the bag of pips and add the sugar, boil fast until the marmalade becomes thick and starts to jelly. Test for the setting point and jar whilst warm.

Grown up Marmalade

Dark, rich and scrumptious with a sophisticated hint of booziness

Ingredients:

1.3kg Seville oranges
2 lemons, juice only
2¼kg granulated or preserving sugar
450g dark muscovado sugar
150ml Amaretto Liqueur or any other liqueur you like

Method:

Place the whole oranges and lemon juice in a large preserving pan and cover with 2 litres/ 4 pints water. If this is not enough to cover the fruit, put it in a smaller pan. If necessary, weight the oranges with a heat-proof plate to keep them under the water. Bring to the boil, cover and simmer very gently for about 2 hours, or until the peel can be pierced easily with a fork.

Warm half of the white and dark sugar in a very low oven. Pour off the cooking water from the oranges into a jug and tip the oranges into a bowl. Return the cooking liquid to the pan. Leave the oranges to cool until they are easy to handle, and then cut them in half. Scoop out all the pips and pith and add these to reserved orange liquid in the pan. Bring to the boil for 6 minutes then strain this liquid through a sieve into a bowl, pressing the pulp through with a wooden spoon; the result is high in pectin, which helps to ensure the marmalade has a good set.

Pour half this liquid into a preserving pan. Cut the peel into chunky shreds, using a sharp knife. Add half the peel to the liquid in the preserving pan with the warm white and dark muscovado sugars. Stir over a low heat until all the sugar has dissolved, then bring to the boil and bubble rapidly for 15-25 minutes until setting point is reached. Stir in half the whisky.

Take the pan off the heat and skim any scum from the surface. (To dissolve any excess scum, drop a small knob of butter on the surface, and gently stir.) Leave the marmalade to stand in the pan for 20 minutes to cool a little and to allow the peel to settle, then pot in sterilised jars, seal and label. Repeat for the remaining batch.

Rhubarb Marmalade

Ingredients:

1.8 kg rhubarb

Grated zest of 5 lemons
340g chopped, blanched almonds
1 tbsp. essence of ginger
2.75kg sugar
18ml water

Method:

Wash the rhubarb and cut into small cubes. Place the fruit in a preserving-pan, with the lemon zest and water and boil it for twenty minutes. Add the blanched almonds, essence of ginger, and sugar and stir continuously until the sugar has fully dissolved. Bring to a rapid boil for twenty minutes or until the marmalade reaches setting point. Ladle into warm jars and seal.

Seville Orange Marmalade

Now thought of as the 'real' or 'traditional' marmalade. This marmalade is made with bitter oranges from the southern Spanish province of Seville which has long been prized for making wonderful marmalade.

Ingredients:

12 large Seville oranges
7.2 litres of water
5.5 kg sugar
Juice of two lemons

Method:

Slice the oranges very thinly. The thinner the slicing the better. Gather all the pips and place them in a cup with a little water and set aside. Place the fruit in a large crock bowl and cover it with the water; cover and leave for twenty-four hours. The next day, boil up the fruit for two hours, adding the liquor from the pips. After two hours the orange rinds should be soft. Add the sugar and stir until fully dissolved. Boil for a further hour and a half, stirring continuously during the last half-hour; add the juice of two lemons, pour the marmalade into pots, and cover it.

Seville Orange Marmalade – another version

Ingredients:

9 large Seville oranges
2 sweet oranges
2 lemons
 5.4 litres of water
4 kg sugar

Method:

Slice all the citrus fruit and thinly as possible and place the fruit in a large bowl and pour over the cold water, leave for twenty-four hours. Gather the pips from all the fruit and put in a small cup with a little water to cover them and set aside overnight. The next day, boil the fruit until tender; add the sugar and stir until it dissolves. Bring back to the boil again, stirring occasionally until the marmalade thickens and sets. Pot up in warm jars and seal.

Strawberry Marmalade

Today's marmalade purists would not consider anything other than preserved citrus fruits to be a marmalade, but this recipe harks back to the days when marmalade recipes included all manner of fruits and was not exclusive to those fruits of a zesty variety.

Ingredients:

1kg strawberries
1 kg sugar
Juice of two lemons
89ml liquid pectin

Method

Crush the strawberries and pass them through a sieve. Place the strawberries and lemon juice in a pan and heat gently for ten minutes, then stir in the sugar, and increase heat to medium-high; bring the mixture to a full rolling boil, stirring constantly. Add the liquid pectin Stir in liquid pectin; return mixture to a full rolling boil, stirring constantly for two minutes. Remove the pan from heat; skim off any foam. To prevent floating fruit, allow marmalade to cool 5 minutes before filling jars. Gently stir the marmalade to distribute the fruit. Ladle the marmalade into hot jars and cover.

Cherry Marmalade

This is a sharp and zingy marmalade that was made for Queen Henrietta Maria, as recorded by her Chancellor Sir Kenelme Digby in his book of 1669, 'The Closet of Sir Kenelme Digby, Kt. Opened'.

Ingredients:

225g raspberries,
1.4kg cherries
225g redcurrants

900g sugar
Juice of 1 lemon

Method:

Wash and stone the cherries. A cherry stoner is a fantastic implement to invest in if this recipe becomes a regular occurrence in your kitchen. Hull the raspberries. Remove the stalks from the redcurrants and rinse them.

Place the raspberries in one saucepan and the redcurrants in another; cover both sets of fruit with water. Bring each to the boil and then simmer for 10 minutes. Allow to cool before straining through a sieve, retaining the juice and discarding the pulp.

Place the prepared cherries into a preserving pan with the redcurrant and raspberry juice. Add the sugar and lemon juice. Stir over a low heat until the sugar has dissolved. Bring to the boil and simmer for about ten minutes and begin checking for the setting point. Once the setting point has been reached pot the marmalade into warm jars and seal immediately.

Chapter Six
Drying

Drying food is an ancient method of preservation, indeed until the introduction of refrigeration dried fruit, vegetables, meat and fish allowed man to survive through seasons of scarcity. Drying fruit, herbs and vegetables is efficient method of storing a glut or a bargain bulk buy. Dried mushrooms, fruits and vegetables are sold in deli's and farm shops with high price labels, but with a bit of time they can be made at home.

Air Drying

Herbs

It is very useful to have a cupboard that is well stocked with dried herbs. A few jars or bunches of dried culinary herbs are an excellent stand-by for adding flavour stews, soups, vegetables, omelettes and well just about any dish you are cooking. Culinary herbs can prove expensive to buy, especially in view of how easy they are to dry and the fact that no special equipment is required.

Always gather the herbs you intend to dry on a warm dry day avoid very hot days (as the sun will evaporate the essential oils) and wet days as this will increase the drying times and can increase the risk of mould developing. Always select the best examples possible, removing dried and damaged leaves before processing.

Tie the herbs in small bunch (process only one variety at a time) and blanch in boiling water for five seconds. Shake of the excess water immediately (a salad spinner is great for this job) and either hang up to air dry or pat dry with a clean cotton tea towel.

Wrap the prepared herbs loosely in pieces of muslin and hang in a warm and dry place. Over a cooker is a good place especially if there is a good level of heat radiating and a draught. Hanging herbs above Ranges such as Aga's and Rayburn's is great for this task and if the heat and draught are good the herbs can be dried in a matter of hours. However, an airing cupboard works well enough, but the absence of a good draught in such places means it will often take 4-5 days to dry the herbs fully.

You will know when the drying process is complete when the leaves are brittle, shed easily and the stems are brittle and crack.

Once dry remove the leaves from the stems, crushing the herbs with a rolling pin. Discarding the stalks and storing the leaves in small airtight bottles or jars. If using clear jars keep them away from direct sunlight in order to retain the colour.

Oven Drying

Dried Fruits and vegetables

Unfortunately we do not have the right Climate in Britain to air dry fruit and vegetables effectively, so you can either use the oven method for drying or use a homemade drying cupboard or purchase a dehydrator.

The oven often seems the most obvious place to start experimenting with drying fruit and vegetables and if you are only planning on doing a few batches of dried goodies a year then the oven is a good option, as whilst not as energy efficient small scale drying doesn't really warrant the expense of a dehydrator or effort of making a drying cabinet.

Slice the fruit and vegetables as thinly as possible, the thinner the slices the quicker they will dry and the better the results will be. A mandolin is great for this task, but I recommend investing in a shield to protect those fingers. Pop fruits such as apples and pears in a solution of lemon juice and water (juice of 1 lemon to 1 pint of water) for a few minutes prior to drying as this will speed up their drying process and give better results.

Drying in the oven takes an average of 7 hours, so choose a day when you have things to get on with in the home but don't need the oven. Turn on your oven as low as it will go (often below the lowest marked setting on your oven) and space the cooking racks evenly apart. cover a few baking sheets with parchment or for larger fruits such as apples and pineapple use wire cooling racks covered with parchment and spread the fruit out in an even layer, pop the baking sheets in the oven, prop the oven door open and set an alarm clock to go off in four hours' time.

At about the four-hour mark, you will start to see signs of shrivelling. At this point you can judge whether you need to flip your fruit or vegetable slices over.

 The fruit will take between seven and eight hours to dry properly and it is a case of using your judgement to decide when it's done. The more moisture you extract the longer the fruit and vegetables will keep.

It will take up a good chunk of your day, but it's almost entirely hands-off.

Mushrooms

When you need to preserve an abundance of mushrooms whether shop-bought or foraged drying is an excellent method to employ and you can get very good results using your home oven.

Most mushrooms dry beautifully, not only retaining but gaining richness of flavour in the process. When rehydrated in hot water, their texture is almost identical to fresh mushrooms. Dried mushrooms can be stored for at least a year, if dried correctly.

Having a good supply of dried mushrooms in the larder is great for using in soups, pasta dishes, stews, breads so many more recipes. Making dried mushrooms is economical and the results are nutritious and delicious.

1. Clean the mushrooms with a brush. Do not wash or peel them. Stubborn dirt can be extracted by using a damp piece of kitchen towel.
2. Slice them thinly; a mandolin can be useful for this. It's important to get thin and even slices as the thicker the slices, the longer the drying process will be.
3. Take two clean cotton tea-towels, placing the mushroom slices in a single layer and covering with the second towel, pat vigorously to remove excess moisture.
4. Arrange the sliced mushrooms on baking sheets in a single layer, ensuring that they do not touch or overlap.
5. Cook at 150oF, 65oC degrees for one hour.
6. Remove the mushrooms from oven and turn over. Using paper towels, blot up any water that has sweated out of the mushrooms. If possible, gently press on the mushroom slices with paper towels to remove any excess water.

7. Return to the oven and cook for another hour.
8. Remove from the oven and let them cool before checking to see if they are crisp and dry. It is important to let the mushrooms cool before checking their consistency as the steam needs to evaporate.
9. When cool the mushrooms should be completely dried. If not, repeat Steps 4 and 5 until they are dry.
10. When the mushrooms are ready there should be no moisture left in them.
11. Dried mushrooms need to be labelled and stored in an air-tight container in a cool, dark place.
12. To use dehydrated mushrooms, pour boiling water over them in a heat-proof bowl. Let them soak for 20 to 30 minutes. Drain and reserve the deeply flavoured soaking liquor using in place of vegetable stock in your recipe.

Dried mushrooms are concentrated in flavour and can be used to compliment any dish that calls for mushrooms. Use the rehydrated mushrooms in recipes where fresh mushrooms could be used. Alternatively grind dried mushrooms with a pinch of sea salt, sprinkling of ground nutmeg and a twist of fresh black pepper to make an excellent seasoning.

Home-Made Drying Cupboard

Purpose made food dehydrators are very effective and give excellent results. They use around 600 watts of electricity and they have controlled thermostats meaning you can achieve consistency in your results. However, the drawer back is that a good one costs around £150-£200. You can build yourself an effective drying cabinet for just over £20 and if you happen to have materials lying around it can cost a lot less.

Make or utilise a wooden box, completely sealing any existing cracks, crevices or holes. Make a door (if it doesn't already have one) to allow you to place your fruit and vegetables in it to dry. Drill some ventilation holes along the top and bottom of the box and install a heat source. A 60 watt light bulb gives the right temperature for a box of 75cm x 45cm x 45 cm.

The trays that are slotted into the box need to be perforated or made from wire to allow effective ventilation and good drying results. If using mesh stretch cheese cloth over the wire shelf and pin it in place to stop the metal mesh from marking the produce. Always wash and dry the cheese-cloth before using, otherwise it imparts a smell and taste that is unpleasant.

Chapter Seven
Blooming Delicious – preserving edible flowers

A Brief History

The history of edible flowers can be traced back thousands of years; indeed Saffron crocuses were first documented over 4000 years ago and arrived in Britain around 3000 years ago. The spice, made from the dried stigmas of the saffron crocus, is still incredibly expensive, because it takes approximately hundred and fifty flowers to yield just 1,000 mg (0.035 oz.) of dry saffron threads and it is an industry that has shunned mechanisation, meaning that the stigmas are still picked by hand.

Until the 18th century it was celebrated for its healing qualities and was dispensed by apothecaries to cure everything from coughs, measles and colds to scabies. The spice was in great demand during the outbreak of the Black Death for its curative and healing qualities and modern research has concluded that it is among the richest plant sources of riboflavin (vitamin B2). It also contains an essential oil, safranal, and some crocetins which are carotenoids, that is to say pro-vitamin A and has many health giving qualities including beneficial effects on immune system helping to reduce the risk of infection.

Saffron has long been prized for its complex flavour which has a semi-sweet, smoky, slightly honeyed flavour;

although some argue that it carries a taste of the sea. As a food dye, saffron was important to Tudor cooks who used it to give a golden hue to pastry, and to give a wonderful rich colour to butter and cream, in Shakespeare's The Winter's Tale, the clown says "I must have saffron to colour the Warden pies". It is still the most expensive spice in the world, and although not regularly used in modern British cuisine it was once so highly prized that it was widely cultivated outdoors in Britain for hundreds of years. Echoes of Britain's saffron growing tradition lives on in place names such as Saffron Walden in Essex & Saffron Hill in East London.

Like Saffron, roses have a long culinary history, with all roses being edible, as the rose and the apple are first cousins. Whilst you can safely eat any colour or type of rose petal different rose varieties have different flavours. Some varieties of roses taste sweet, while others taste slightly sour or even spicy. Generally the more scented the rose the better it will taste. Rose petals can be used in salads, confectionary, and desserts as well as in home preserves such as jellies, butters and syrups.

Roses first came to the West from Persia in 1240 by way of French Crusaders. The first known cultivated rose is Rosa gallica var. officinalis, also known as the apothecary rose, which gives an indication of the fact that roses were originally prized for their medicinal virtues.

Rosewater which is the distilled essence of rose flowers and commonly used in puddings, cakes, biscuits, jellies and syrups was invented as early as the 3rd and 4th century. According to the Oxford Companion to Food, It was used as a flavouring and medicinal element in ancient Egypt, Greece, Rome, Persia and South Asia.

Roses even helped the war effort, as during World War II, when citrus fruits were not available due to shortages, the Ministry of Food sent people out into the countryside to gather rose hips from wild hedgerow roses to make into syrup and take as a vitamin C supplement. If you look at a rose hip you can see a strong resemblance to an immature apple.

Bright, cheerful and butterfly-like nasturtium blossoms have also delighted gardeners and cooks alike for centuries. The leaves are spicy, bittersweet with a peppery kick. Nasturtiums are mentioned in Apicius, a cookbook from ancient Rome, indicating their long standing status as a food ingredient. Indeed, Nasturtium seeds were apparently used as a substitute for black pepper during WWII, although roasted nasturtium seeds are reported to smell like old men's trousers.

Throughout history a variety of edible flowers have been utilised by cooks to add colour and flavour to dishes. Hugh Platt's 1602 book 'Delights for Ladies', includes recipes for crystallising flowers. It was common for violets, cowslips, pinks, roses, and marigolds to be used as natural food colourings during the Renaissance.

The Victorian Era was the original age of flower power, with edible flowers enjoying great popularity, especially as part of salads. The Victorians added violets, borage, primroses, gilly flowers (clove pinks) and nasturtiums to salads and garnishes for both aesthetics and flavour. The Victorians were fond of making flower syrups, cordials and jams as a way of preserving the flowers for the winter months. They also crystallised violets, roses and other flowers to garnish cakes and confectionary.

Flowers can require patience to work with. The delicate flowers and flower petals can quickly wilt or become damaged if they are cooked too long or drenched in dressing, but they are well worth taking time over as they can add a splash of elegance and flavour to the plainest of sponges or ordinary dish.

The Edible Flower Commandments

1. Positively Identify - make sure you know what you are eating. Consult a good reference book for a comprehensive list of edible flowers. It is easy for beginners to make mistakes as not all flowers in the same family are edible for example, Day lilies (Hemerocallis species) are edible, and all other lilies (Asiatic, Oriental) are not. The flowers from garden peas are edible; however, sweet pea flowers (Lathyrus spp.) are not edible. Tuberous begonia flowers are edible; however, wax begonia flowers (Begonia semperflorens) are not edible.

2. Consume in moderation. When starting to incorporate edible flowers into your cooking start off with small amounts to see how your body reacts to them, even edible flowers can upset some people's digestion.

3. Taste before adding to a dish. Even if a flower is edible and it agrees with your digestive system, it doesn't mean it will be agreeable to your palette. Taste a few of your selected blooms before adding them to any of your recipes to be certain you will enjoy the flavour.

4. Avoid harvesting edible flowers from the side of the road where they may be contaminated from harmful exhaust fumes.

5. Do not harvest flowers in the wild unless you have permission from the land owner and are absolutely certain of their identification.

6. Certain flowers in the composite family (chamomile, chrysanthemum, daisies, and sunflowers) should be avoided by people with asthma, hay fever sufferers and those with allergies. The presence of large amounts of pollen in these types of flowers may produce an allergic reaction in people with sensitive systems.

7. You should only use organically grown flowers. Flowers obtained from garden centres and florists are probably not safe to eat. The flowers you use must be free from any harmful chemicals such as chemical pesticides.

8. As a general rule, you should use only the flower petals of edible flowers, however, flowers such as violets, pansies and primroses can be consumed whole, just be certain to remove the green sepal from the base of the flower before using.

9. Always pick flowers early in the morning after the dew has dried on them or in the early evening. Flowers that are picked during the heat of midday will quickly wilt or dry out before you have a chance to use them.

10. Only select the best specimens for use in culinary preparation and preserving.

Preparing flowers to eat

1. Remove the pistils and stamens from the flowers if present and also gently remove any residual pollen with a small, soft brush. Some flowers such as daisies, marigolds, clove pinks and roses have a bitter white heel that is present at the base of each petal. Remove

this heel prior to adding these types of flowers to your culinary explorations for the best possible flavour.

2. Gently wash the flowers if any dirt or insects are present. Carefully pat the flowers dry with kitchen towel or use a salad spinner to remove any excess water.

3. The harvested and cleaned flowers should be used immediately or stored by placing the flowers in a plastic food bag or air-tight plastic container such as a lunch-box, along with one or two moist paper towels and stored in the refrigerator. Flowers with longer stems can be placed in a vase of water, which can then be placed inside the refrigerator until needed.

Crystallising Flowers

Crystallised flowers add a touch of elegance to cakes and confectionary. Flowers that are suitable for crystallising include: Violets; Nasturtiums; Lavender flowers; Rose petals; Small rosebuds; Small mint leaves; Rosemary flowers and Primrose flowers. They will keep quite happily in an airtight tin, in a cool, dry and dark place, for around two months. If you need to keep them longer you will need to use gum tragacanth.

Ingredients:

Egg white
Caster sugar
2 tbsp. water
Small, soft
Soft paint brush
Edible flowers

Directions:

Place the clean dry flowers on a flat surface.

Fork through the egg white to a light foam and whisk in 2 tbsp. water. Brush the flowers all over with beaten egg white, using a soft brush.

Sprinkle flowers all over with the caster sugar immediately. The sugar needs to stick to the egg white before it dries.

Leave for approximately one hour or more until fully set and crisp.

You can also sit the finished flowers on a baking tray lined with ovenproof paper in a warm oven (switched off).

Re-apply the egg white and sprinkle over more sugar

Check for any uncovered areas and reapply where necessary

Leave to dry for 12-24 hours.

Once hardened they will keep for a month in an airtight tin. If you want them to last longer, you'll need to use a different technique. Put two tablespoons of rosewater and one teaspoon of gum tragacanth (also called gum Arabic) in a jar, shake them up together and leave the mixture for 24 hours in a warm place. Coat the flowers using a fine brush then follow the instructions above. They will last for a few months in an airtight tin.

Tips

Leave the stalks on small flowers such as violets as it makes it easier to handle them

Use a flour sifter to help coat the flowers with sugar evenly.

Cocktail sticks are helpful to manoeuvre flowers once they are coated.

Lightly grind the caster sugar in a mortar and pestle or pulse a couple of times in a food processor as the slightly finer sugar gives better results.

Common Edible Flowers

This list is by no means comprehensive, but it provides a good starting point for beginning to cook, preserve and eat edible flowers.

- Cottage pink (Dianthus caryophyllus) – has a spicy, clove-like flavour and is referred to as gilliflower in old recipe books. This flower was the basis for a popular Elizabethan drink known as Gilliflower Water.

- Daylily (Hemerocallis fulva) – add the petals or buds to salads

- Marigold (Calendula officinalis) – this is the pot, or English marigold, sometimes called poor man's saffron

- Nasturtium (Tropaeolum majus) – the bright flowers and green leaves have a peppery kick.

- Pansy (Viola) – great for crystallising and also look pretty set in jellies and ice cubes

- Rose (Rosa) – Excellent for making butter creams, fondant fillings, crystallising, syrups, jellies and the petals freeze well in ice-cubes.

- Sunflower (Helianthus annuus) – use either the petals themselves or the unopened buds. They have a sharp, slightly bitter flavour.

- Dill and fennel – a delicate lacy look and a mild aniseed flavour ideal in fish dishes.

- Borage – vivid blue, has a hint of cucumber and is a great addition to summer drinks, scrambled eggs and salads.

- Basil, mint, rosemary and thyme – all work well sprinkled over salads as well as made into jellies. Work well sprinkled on pasta dishes.

- Lavender – ideal for flavouring sugar, baking, ice-creams, syrups and jellies.

Rose and Strawberry Jam

There is something quintessentially British about this flavoursome recipe with floral tones.

Ingredients:

8 red or pink roses (scented)
1 kg strawberries (hulled and quartered)
800 gram(s) jam sugar
Juice and zest of 1 lemon
30 mls rose water

Method

Remove the petals from the roses and wash in cold water. Remove the bitter white base from the petals. Place the strawberries in a preserving pan with the sugar. Set the pan over a low heat to allow the sugar to dissolve slowly, stirring constantly with a wooden spoon. Once the sugar has completely dissolved, increase the heat and bring the jam to the boil. Boil rapidly over a medium heat for about 20 minutes stirring from time to time until the mixture has begun to thicken.

Test for a set and keep checking every 4 minutes for a set.

Once the jam has reached setting point add the lemon juice, rose water and rose petals and cook for a further 2-3 minutes. Remove from the heat and allow to rest for 5 minutes before ladling into prepared jars.

Primrose and Cardamom Curd

A delicate floral curd with the deeply aromatic flavour of cardamom, this is well worth making.

Ingredients

A generous handful of washed primrose petals
450g sugar
450g cooking apples
125g unsalted butter
5 large eggs, lightly beaten
4 cardamom pods
The zest and juice of 2 lemons

Method

The day before you want to make the curd, gather your primroses, finely chop the petals and place them with the sugar in an airtight container. Cover and leave for at least 24 hours.

The next day stir the primrose infused sugar and set aside. Peel and chop the apples and place them into a pan with 100ml of water, cardamom seeds and the lemon zest.

On a low heat gently cook the apple until it is soft and pulpy, then mash to a purée

Set a bowl over a pan of boiling water. Add the apple purée, butter, lemon juice and primrose sugar to the bowl. Stir the mixture until the butter has completely melted.

Turn off the heat and add the eggs gradually to the mixture, whisking continually.

Return the pan to a gentle heat and stir the mixture continually with a wooden spoon, for about 10 minutes or until it thickens. Pour the curd into sterilised jars, seal immediately and store in the fridge, where it will keep for up to a month.

Rose Petal Jelly

This is a preserve pièce de résistance, its subtle floral tones, sweet brilliance and tender pink hues set it apart from other jellies.

Ingredients

1 litre dog rose petals
1 litre water
juice of two lemons
1 kilo sugar

Method

Pull the petals of the stem and loosely fill a one-litre measuring jug. Wash under running cold water. Place the petals in a stainless steel saucepan with a litre of water, bring to the boil and simmer for 15 minutes. The roses will completely lose their colour, and the water will turn murky reddish brown, this is normal. Strain the liquid into a non-metallic bowl and allow to cool.

Next add the lemon juice to the cooled rose water and watch the murky brown water transform into a beautiful, bright pink. Pour the liquid back into the pan, and add one kilo of preserving sugar. When the sugar has disappeared, turn up the heat a little and bring to the boil. It will take 10 minutes to reach setting point if using preserving sugar, if not using preserving sugar you will need to add pectin to achieve a set.

Skim the jelly and then ladle into sterilised jars.

Violet Syrup

A brilliant purple syrup that is ideal for drizzling over cheesecakes and ice-creams. Its scent can be enhanced by adding a drop of pure essential oil of sweet orange oil or neroli at the point of bottling.

Ingredients

500g   clean, tightly packed fresh Violet flowers.
750ml water
2kg white sugar

Method:

Place Violet flowers in a Pyrex, crock or enamelled pot with lid.

In a separate pan bring the water to a boil. Pour the water over the Violet Flowers and cover tightly.

Allow to steep overnight at room temperature .After a minimum of 14 hours, press out as much of the liquid as you can. (a clean pair of tight is useful in this process).

Measure out your purple liquid and put it through a very coffee filter or piece of muslin.

Add your liquid to a clean saucepan.

For every 100ml of liquid add 200g of sugar.

Bring slowly to a boil on medium heat stirring continually until the sugar dissolves.

Skim of the scum as it collects.

DO NOT LET IT COME TO A FULL BOIL and DO NOT ADD LEMON JUICE AS IT WILL IMPAIR THE COLOUR.

Take it off the heat,

Wait for 5 minutes and repeat the process. Again, stirring, but not allowing to boil. Take it off the heat. Decant into sterilised bottles or jars.

Wartime Rosehip Syrup

This is a wonderful wartime recipe from The Hedgerow Harvest, Ministry of Food , 1943. When food was short during the Second World War every possible edible resource had to be utilised and the MoF issued these instructions for making rosehip syrup out of about 2 pounds (900gm) of rosehips.

Method

Boil 3 pints (1.7 litres) of boiling water.

Mince the hips in a course mincer and pour immediately into the boiling water.

Bring to boil and then place aside for 15 minutes.

Pour into a flannel or linen crash jelly bag and allow to drip until the bulk of the liquid has come through.

Return the residue to the saucepan, add one and a half pints (852ml) of boiling water, stir and allow to stand for 10 minutes.

Pour back into the jelly bag and allow to drip through. To make sure all the sharp hairs are removed, put back the first half cupful of liquid and allow to drip through again.

Put the mixed juice into a clean saucepan and boil down until the juice measures about one and a half pints (852ml), then add one and a quarter pounds (560gm) of sugar and boil for a further 5 minutes.

Pour into hot sterile bottles and seal at once.

Tips

- If corks are used, these should have been boiled for an hour just previously and after insertion.
- It is advisable to use small bottles as the syrup will not keep for more than a week or two once the bottle is opened.
- Store in a dark cupboard.

Modern Recipe for Rosehip Syrup

This is a modern redaction of the Ministry of Foods recipe and can be used as a cordial, interesting addition to rice pudding or sauce for ice cream.

Ingredients

1kg rosehips
3 litres of water
500g light brown soft sugar

Method:

Bring to the boil 2 litres of water.

Chop the rosehips and mash them by placing in a thick carrier bag and bashing with a rolling pin, place the prepared rosehips in a preserving pan and add to boiling water.

Bring the water back to the boil, then remove from heat and allow to steep for an hour.

Pour rosehips and liquid into a scalded jelly bag and allow the juice to drip through. This will take several hours. Do not squeeze the jelly bag as this will make the syrup cloudy.

Add rosehip pulp back to a saucepan containing 1 litre of water and bring to the boil. Then remove from heat and allow the contents to steep for an hour before straining through the jelly bag as in the previous step.

Add the sugar to the combined strained rosehip liquid and stir until the sugar has dissolved, allow to simmer for five minutes, and then pour into hot, sterilised bottles. Keep in the fridge.

Chapter Eight
Preserving in Wartime

With the British love of jam and marmalade being so strong it was going to take more than a war to stop us enjoying our morning toast with preserves. During the Second World War, your preserve ration was one pound of jam per person every two months; this meagre ration could be supplemented with home-made preserves and if you surrendered your preserve ration you could get a little extra sugar to make your own preserves, and with the ration value being so low making your own instead was a good idea. Even with a little extra sugar on hand the success of preserve making was dependent on having a supply of fresh, locally grown fruit. Before the War most of our fruit was imported so from 1939 to 1945 fresh fruit was in short supply (and in some cases such as bananas virtually impossible to get). Many of the pre-war recipes for soft fruit jams and orange marmalades were now replaced with recipes for preserves that made the most of readily available ingredients such as rhubarb, carrots and even parsley. It is certain that the secret to success in a wartime kitchen was undoubtedly that of ingenuity and adaptation.

War Time Rhubarb Jam

Ingredients

2 lbs Rhubarb
2 lbs Sugar

Method:

Wash the rhubarb and chop into inch long pieces. Place into a large non-metallic bowl and cover with the sugar, cover the bowl with a clean tea-towel and leave to steep overnight.

The next morning pour the rhubarb and sugar into a preserving pan and prepare for a slow and long cook. Heat gently stirring until the sugar has dissolved. When stirring avoid mashing or crushing the rhubarb pieces as it is nice to have chunks of intact fruit in the jam. Bring to a rapid boil for eight minutes and then test for the setting point, once the setting point has been reached pot immediately. Should keep for twelve months.

Mixed Fruit Jam

With fruit being in short supply mixed fruit jams became popular in the 1940's as people collected together hedgerow gluts and fruit from their gardens making a delicious taste of summer in a jar.

Ingredients:

2lbs of mixed berries (strawberries, blackberries, bilberries, raspberries, elderberries, red and black currants all work well)
1 lb of sugar
2 tablespoons of water

Method

Add the fruit to the preserving pan with the sugar and water and set over a low heat. Gently bring to a gentle simmer and stir to dissolve the sugar, cook gently for twenty minutes, stirring occasionally to prevent sticking.

Bring to a rapid boil for five minutes. Test for the setting point. This recipe does not include added pectin or lemon juice and so a long so cook is required to get a set.

Make Do and Mend Carrot Jam

Ingredients

8 oz peeled cooked carrots, pulped.
1 lb of apples peeled, cored and cooked in ¼ pint of water until they are reduced to a pulp
¼ tsp almond essence
1 lb sugar

Method

Combine the carrot and apple pulp in a preserving pan and add the sugar. Stir over a medium heat until the sugar has dissolved and then boil until the mixture thickens, this will not set like standard jams. Pot and consume within two months.

It just goes to show that no matter how hard times are there is always a passion for preserves and always a way of getting your jam fix.

Bibliography:

Classical Dictionary of the Vulgar Tongue, second Edition, 1811, London.

The Rise of the Marmalade Dynasty, 1800 – 1879 (ISBN 0 900019 34 4).Dr. William Mathew

The Secret History of Guernsey Marmalade: James Keiller & Son Offshore (ISBN 0 9532547 0 4), Dr William Mathew

Mrs. Beetons Book of Household Management, abridged edition, Isabella Beeton, Oxford University Press, 2008 , ISBN-10   0199536333

Apicius: A Critical Edition with an Introduction and English Translation Apicius (Author), Christopher Grocock (Author), Sally Grainger (Author) Publication date 2006 | ISBN-10: 1903018137

Oxford English Dictionary, published 2010 ISBN-10: 0199571120

The Book of Marmalade (The English Kitchen) C. Anne Wilson, 2010, ISBN-10: 1903018773

Cooking in Europe 1650-1850 (Greenwood Press Daily Life Through History Series) Ivan Day, 2008, ISBN-13: 978-0313346248

Romeo and Juliet (Wordsworth Classics) Edition 7, 2000, ISBN-13: 978-1840224337

English Recipes and Others From Scotland, Wales and Ireland
Sheila Hutchins, 1967

Fruit & Health, (Fruit Trades' Federation, London, EC4)

The National Mark Calendar of Cooking (Compiled for the
Ministry of Agriculture by Ambrose Heath + D.D.
Cottington-Taylor, 1936)

Vegetable & Fruit Dishes, Madam F. Nietlispack, John
Hamilton Ltd